PRAISE FOR
AROUND THE WORLD IN 69 DAYS

"Congratulations on completing your round the world flight"

Fredrick W. Smith
Chairman and President of FedEx Corporation

"Although this book is interwoven with aviation themes and metaphors of how human courage can overcome obstacles and challenges, a greater undertone of the book is the amazing story of China, as told through the eyes of this young man, his mom, his community and his dream. The emergence of China in the past 30 years and its re-entry to the family of the nations of the world is perhaps of the greatest forces at play in the 21st century. Wei, you have told that story with power, personal touch and an authenticity which our world so desperately needs."

Shane Tedjarati,
President of Global High Growth Regions at Honeywell

"Around The World in 69 Days is an inspiration to everybody that seeks achievement in those things that have not been done before. It is especially noteworthy for those of us who love to fly small airplanes but only dream of flying around the world or be the first to accomplish a new record flight as Wei Chen has done. Best wishes it is an honor to be your friend!"

Larry Cox
President of Memphis Airport Authority

"This story about Wei's trip around the world is a testimate to Wei's energy and passion for forming close relationships and friendships and inspiring people to persevere and be their very best. Throughout the trip, Wei inspired many entrepreneurs and business leaders in the Young Presidents Organization to be part of his historic journey."

Steve Sansom
YPO/WPO International Board of Directors

"The author, Wei Chen, is a man of this new, fast changing, world we live in. This book exhibits broad insight into our world as it exists today, as well as the social, industrial, and humanitarian changes likely coming tomorrow. A great adventure that asks, 'What would you attempt to do if you knew you could not fail?'"

Elgen M. Long
Aviator; Earthrounder, 1971

"The story of Wei Chen's amazing journey is a true testament to the power of discipline and focus—and truly inspires all of us to think bigger and execute better!"

Verne Harnish
Author of *Mastering the Rockefeller Habits* and
The Greatest Business Decisions of All Time

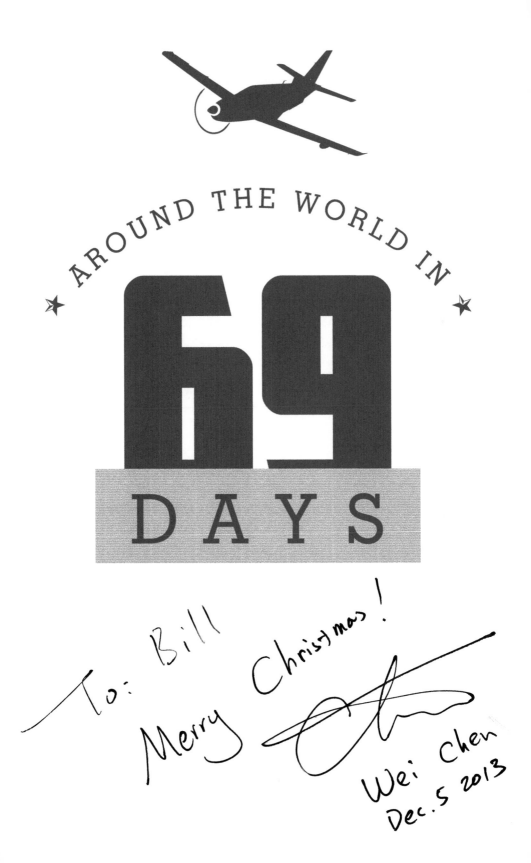

AROUND THE WORLD IN

69

DAYS

To: Bill
Merry Christmas!

Wei Chen
Dec. 5 2013

AROUND THE WORLD IN

69

DAYS

WHAT WOULD YOU ATTEMPT TO DO
IF YOU KNEW YOU **COULD NOT FAIL?**

WEI CHEN

Advantage.

Published by Advantage, Charleston, South Carolina.
Member of Advantage Media Group.

ADVANTAGE is a registered trademark and the Advantage colophon is a trademark of Advantage Media Group, Inc.

Printed in the United States of America.

ISBN: 978-1-59932-402-9
LCCN: 2013949194

This publication is designed to provide accurate and authoritative information in regard to the subject matter covered. It is sold with the understanding that the publisher is not engaged in rendering legal, accounting, or other professional services. If legal advice or other expert assistance is required, the services of a competent professional person should be sought.

Advantage Media Group is proud to be a part of the Tree Neutral® program. Tree Neutral offsets the number of trees consumed in the production and printing of this book by taking proactive steps such as planting trees in direct proportion to the number of trees used to print books. To learn more about Tree Neutral, please visit www.treeneutral.com. To learn more about Advantage's commitment to being a responsible steward of the environment, please visit www.advantagefamily.com/green

TreeNeutral

Advantage Media Group is a publisher of business, self-improvement, and professional development books and online learning. We help entrepreneurs, business leaders, and professionals share their Stories, Passion, and Knowledge to help others Learn & Grow. Do you have a manuscript or book idea that you would like us to consider for publishing? Please visit advantagefamily.com or call 1.866.775.1696.

I dedicate this book to my mom, who didn't have the opportunity to finish high school and who worked as a factory laborer, starting at 11 years of age. She never complained and always had the most positive attitude possible, even during challenging times. She gave birth to me when she was only 17, at the height of China's Cultural Revolution. Even when we didn't have enough food or clothes, she instilled a sense of pride in me. She encouraged me not to give up on my education. She was proud of me, whether I was a rebellious child fighting in the streets or a successful entrepreneur.

I dedicate this book also to my three precious daughters, Elisabeth, Stephanie, and Sabrina. They are the reason I wrote it.

My final dedication is to my smarter, better half, Isabel, who always supports me unconditionally and says "Yes" to every crazy dream I have – even when I have no clue how to accomplish one.

TABLE OF CONTENTS

INTRODUCTION

Two roads diverged in a wood, and I took the one less traveled by, and that has made all the difference.

- Robert Lee Frost

'm afraid to write a book. I am more afraid to write a book that's just about flying around the world.

It's not writing that I fear. I've written many magazine articles. However, in this story, I want readers to find something valuable to apply to their own lives. I have struggled with a book focused on flying, as I am not the most experienced aviator. I had less than 500 flight hours when I started the trip to fly around the world.

A friend asked me what my kids thought about this trip, and I told him they were too young to understand. Then it struck me that I might not remember details about the flight when they grow older. I wouldn't be able to answer all their intelligent questions when they were old enough to ask. I wrote this book to help them understand what I did and why I did it. I wanted them to feel proud of their dad's accomplishment, just as I want other readers to find even the smallest inspiration to pursue their own audacious dreams. One of my favorite books is Meg Meeker's *Strong Fathers, Strong Daughters*, which holds that a father is the most important man in his daughter's life. Daughters need strong fathers to become strong in their own lives.

This is *not* a book about how to fly around the world. It is about identifying your "Big Hairy Audacious Goal" and finding a way to accomplish it through focus and discipline. I share my life experiences and hope to encourage readers to dream big and turn dreams to reality.

I divide my flight into eight segments. In each, I bring out my life stories: my childhood during China's tumultuous Cultural Revolution, coming to the U.S. for higher education, starting a company, and my passion for flying. These stories evolve from one question: "What would you attempt to do if you knew you could not fail?"

I feel extremely blessed. The events described in this book took place when I was 40. I'm writing two years later, after accomplishing my three wildest dreams: coming to the U.S. and getting an MBA degree when I hardly spoke English; starting a company and becoming a millionaire when I had no capital, no business plan, no investors, no social network, and no experience; and becoming the first Chinese citizen to fly a single-engine airplane around the world when I had barely 500 hours of flight time over a mere four years.

What is your dream? "What would you attempt to do if you knew you could not fail?"

I am a fan of Jim Collins. My favorite books are his *Good to Great* and *Great by Choice*, which he coauthored with Morten T. Hansen. His theories helped me grow in both business and personal endeavors. His theories even helped me complete the flight successfully. I've incorporated many of his business theories in this book – the Big Hairy Audacious Goal, the Hedgehog Concept, the 20 Mile March, Fire Bullets, then Cannonballs, Return on Luck, the Culture of Discipline, and many others.

The most frequently asked question about the trip is: "Were you alone during the whole flight?" I was fortunate that I was never alone. I had four co-pilots for different segments – Rob Williams, Alan Hepburn, Claude Chiffaut, and Chris Hare – and I had 22 passengers who joined me for different portions of the trip. Some were pre-arranged, including my wife Isabel; my father; my brother, Andy Chen; my "brother from another mother," John Chen; Earl Blankenship; Lawson and Cynthia Baker; Samer Baassiri; Jason Zhang; Binling Wu; Linda Lin, Tricia Montgomery and Doug Day. Some were strangers I met along the way: Simon Bai and Guanhua Liu from Barcelona; Zhixiao Dong, who I met in Greece; a China Central Television (CCTV) cameraman, Zheng Chang, and news reporter from Beijing, Li Ye; Shawn and Grace from Seattle; and Yuzhong Ma from Oshkosh, to name a few. In cities with large Chinese communities, such as Washington, D.C., Toronto, Paris, Madrid, Barcelona, Milan, Rome, Dubai, Bangkok, Vientiane, Ho Chi Minh City, Hong Kong, and all of the stops in China, there were 20 to 300 Chinese people welcoming me in the airports. They gave me flowers and said they were proud of what I was trying to accomplish. They hosted receptions, gave me hugs and wished me luck on the journey.

I am humbled and deeply touched by their enthusiasm. I came to realize this was not just a trip for me, but one that touched the lives of thousands of Chinese people worldwide. I felt their pride that a Chinese national was able to fly a private airplane around the world, an unthinkable accomplishment in earlier times, before China's advance to become the world's second largest economy.

I was born in 1971, during China's Cultural Revolution, when most Chinese people did not have enough to eat. My 40-year life reflects the country's stunning achievements during that time. Without China's growth, I would not have been able to accomplish my "American Dream" and become a self-made millionaire in less than ten years. Without China's growth, I would not have been able to afford flying, much less flying around the world. Chinese people were proud of my trip, but more importantly, they were proud of what China has become. I carried a small message.

The Chinese government also gave me tremendous support. Not only did it arrange a news conference in Beijing on March 9, 2011, to announce the trip to Chinese communities worldwide, but it also sent a troupe of 17 performers to celebrate the trip in Madrid, Barcelona, and Rome.

To me a huge milestone was landing at Beijing Capital International Airport, a first for a privately piloted, single-engine airplane. This would not have been possible without the help of many friends. Special thanks go to Hawk Yang, a pioneer and respected leader in promoting general aviation in China. His determination helped keep my dream alive. Thanks to his encouragement, I didn't give up on what others told me was impossible. Through his efforts and connections, I got a permit to land at Beijing Capital International

Airport. Tragically, I lost this dear friend just three months after I came to know him. He drowned during a river adventure on June 18, 2011, at the age of 40, while I was flying around the world. His support enabled my landing at Beijing Capital International Airport, but he didn't live to see it. I realize how blessed I was to survive the challenges I faced and accomplish this mission.

Me and my partner

CHAPTER ONE

BIG HAIRY
AUDACIOUS GOAL
(DEPARTURE DAY)

He who is not courageous enough to take risks
will accomplish nothing in life.

- Muhammad Ali

About seven in the morning on May 22, 2011, the day I was to begin my flight, the phone rang, waking me. I'd been out late the night before at a fundraiser for St. Jude Children's Research Hospital, which was the kick-off for my around-the-world adventure. The skies were clear last night, but by morning a rain storm had hit Memphis. I could hear thunder, as I reached for the phone. It was Thierry Pouille, a French pilot who'd helped me plot my flight.

"Wei, terrible news. There's been a volcanic eruption in Iceland. It doesn't look good." He went on to tell me that the volcano, Grímsvötn, had erupted on the evening of May 21, 2011, and was sending billows of ash as high as 12 km, resulting in the cancellation of 900 flights. The eruption was much larger than that of Iceland's Eyjafjallajökull on April 14, 2010.

My heart sank. Was this going to be a repeat of what happened last spring? The eruption of Eyjafjallajökull caused the largest air-traffic shutdown since World War II. Millions of passengers were stranded, not only in Europe but worldwide. In Europe alone, more than 107,000 flights were cancelled over eight days, affecting 48 percent of air traffic and roughly 10 million passengers. The International Air Transport Association (IATA) estimated the cost to the global airline industry at $200 million a day, for a total of about $1.7 billion.

Volcanic ash was a huge danger that could clog my airplane's single engine. In 1982, British Airways flight 9 flew through volcanic ash of Mount Galunggung, Java, Indonesia, causing four engines to temporarily shut down. For my trip, Iceland was a must-stop because of my airplane's limited range. I could fly nonstop for only four and a half hours with a maximum range of 1,200 nautical miles. For me to fly from Canada to Europe, a stop in Greenland and Iceland couldn't be avoided, as the total distance is more than 2,000 nautical miles. If I had engine failure, there were only two possibilities: ditch the airplane in the freezing ocean or crash land on a mountain of ice. Even if I survived an off-field landing, I would have frozen to death before a rescue team could find me. The chance of survival was zero.

The night before, everything had been perfect, including the weather. One of my goals for this trip was to raise money for St. Jude, my favorite charity. The hospital's mission is to make sure "No child is denied treatment based on race, religion or a family's inability to pay." It provides free treatment to any child who has a referral, based on eligibility as part of a current treatment study. The work they do is magic.

We organized a black tie send-off in the hangar of Wilson Air Center benefiting St. Jude, and about 400 people attended. The pricey tickets sold out. Many generous sponsors were from the Memphis community; others were from around the world, including many friends from China. We were able to raise close to $100,000 that night through live auctions and silent auctions. We had a martial arts performance, dancing, and delicious food. Everyone gave me their best wishes and blessings for the trip.

My mom and dad flew from China for the event, and my lovely wife of course was with me. Only my children, who were seven, three and one, couldn't come. They didn't know much about what I was planning. I had explained a little of it to them, but the undertaking was too big for them to grasp. All they knew was that they wouldn't see Dad for a while.

The volcanic eruption came as a shock that jeopardized my 18 months of planning. Would a mountain in Iceland derail my dream of becoming the first Chinese citizen to fly a single-engine plane around the world?

That dream was born on one not-so-busy night in the fall of 2009. I was lying in bed with my laptop researching adventurous trips and fun places I could fly to. I came across a website that had the records of all individuals who had flown around the world in single-engine airplanes, twin-engine airplanes, helicopters, and other aircraft. After putting our two kids to bed, Isabel walked into the bedroom. Half joking and half serious, I asked her, "What would you think about me flying my airplane around the world?"

As supportive as she always is, she didn't hesitate. She said, "Great!" Boy, she didn't realize her one word would lead to days of research and an obsession with this Big Hairy Audacious Goal. I found out that fewer than 170 people had accomplished it since 1924, and no Chinese citizen had ever done it. That was my biggest inspiration.

Through research, I discovered that, for powered aviation, a round-the-world flight must meet the following criteria to count as an official record:

- Start and finish at the same point and cross all meridians.

- Cover at least 36,787.559 kilometers (22,858.729 miles), which is the length of the Tropic of Cancer. (That is, the most northerly circle of latitude at which the Sun appears directly overhead at its zenith.)

- The course must include control points at latitudes outside the Arctic and Antarctic circles.

The first successful flight around the world started in Seattle, Washington, on April 6, 1924. The team of pilots started with four specially made airplanes, and included Major Frederick Martin, Lieutenant Lowell H. Smith, 1st Lieutenant Leigh P. Wade, and Lieutenant Erik Nelson. The airplanes were built by the Douglas Aircraft Company, which was awarded the contract just 45 days before they delivered the first plane. The airplanes were named Seattle, Chicago, Boston and New Orleans.

The lead plane, Seattle, crashed in dense fog near Port Moller, Alaska on April 30, 1924. The Boston was forced to make an emergency landing in the Atlantic due to oil problems on August 2, 1924. It sank while being towed for repairs. Crews of both planes were rescued.

The surviving planes entered United States airspace on September 8, 1924, and the nation was becoming increasingly excited that they would indeed fly around the world. The crews made stops at various cities before landing in Seattle on September 28, 1924.

The trip had taken 175 days, and covered 27,553 miles (44,085 km). The Douglas Aircraft Company adopted the motto, "First Around the World – First the World Around."

When I started planning the trip, I was a rookie pilot, with less than 200 hours flying time, just two years' worth of flight experience. Circumnavigating the globe really was a Big Hairy Audacious Goal for me. I'd been flying different airplanes, but when I first conceived of this dream to fly around the world, by no standard could I have been considered a seasoned pilot. Many experienced pilots considered my attempt "suicidal." Why did I want to do this when I had such little experience? Why not wait a few years?

One inspiration to attempt this Mount Everest of flying came from Jim Collins. His wife, Joanne Ernst, began racing marathons and triathlons in the early 1980s. She had success in a race with many of the world's best woman triathletes and managed to finish in the top ten. A few weeks later, she told Jim quietly and calmly, "I think I could win the Ironman."

The Ironman, the world championship of triathlons, involves 2.4 miles of ocean swimming, 112 miles of cycling, and ends with a 26.2-mile marathon through lava fields on the Kona coast of Hawaii. Joanne found her Big Hairy Audacious Goal and discovered her personal Hedgehog Concept: She had the passion, she had the genetics and, if she won races, she'd have the economics. Three years later, on a hot October day in 1985, she crossed the finish line at the Hawaii Ironman World Championship in first place.

After reading that story, I asked myself, what is my Big Hairy Audacious Goal? I knew it right away: to fulfill my dream of becoming the first Chinese citizen to fly a single-engine plane around the world. And what was my personal Hedgehog Concept to make this happen? I had a passion for aviation; I had the skills to pilot an airplane and arrange the logistics; and if I accomplished this mission, I'd have the honor of being in Chinese aviation history, forever.

When I started planning, I realized the difficulties it would present. It wasn't just about flying. That's only a part of the challenge. Taking off, landing, and flying were all pretty routine. A big problem turned out to be red tape. There are a lot more restrictions on a Chinese citizen to fly around the world than on Westerners because we need a visa for every country we go to.

I had to apply for 12 visas for 16 countries – Greenland, the United Kingdom, Cyprus, Saudi Arabia, UAE, Oman, India, Thailand, Laos, Vietnam, Russia – and one Schengen visa for five countries: Iceland, France, Spain, Italy, Greece. I did not need a visa for Canada, Hong Kong, and China. Getting the visas was not even the biggest challenge. It was the timing of the applications. Most countries would allow only 90 days to enter once a visa was issued, so I had less than that time to get visas for all of the countries I needed to enter.

I sent applications for India and Oman in January 2011. When my passport came back with the visas, both entries were dated April 2011. I wouldn't depart from Memphis until May 22, so I had to apply again. Other countries such as the U.K. would take a minimum of two weeks. To fully utilize the 90 days, I needed to schedule each application carefully. I applied for my U.K. visa in March, so I could enter in late May. I made my final application for Russia in the middle of May, so I could enter in mid-July. I didn't get my passport back until May 21, 2011, the day before my departure date. I still didn't have time to get visas for Greenland, United Arab Emirates, and Thailand. I could get a "visa on arrival" for UAE and Thailand. Avoiding application errors that could have led to lost time was a tremendous challenge and required strict attention to detail. Keeping track of every bureaucratic requirement was a Big Hairy Audacious Goal in itself.

Aside from securing visas, the bigger challenge was the limited range of the airplane. I'd have to stop at many small airports, some of which were in inhospitable regions. To cross the Atlantic and Pacific Oceans, I had to fly along the coastline of four continents and find airports within my airplane's cruise range.

When I started planning the trip, I had a Piper Saratoga, which was the same type of airplane that John F. Kennedy, Jr. crashed into the Atlantic Ocean on July 16, 1999, killing himself, his wife, and his sister-in-law. The range of a Saratoga was only 850 nautical miles. Its maximum cruise ceiling was 20,000 feet, but since the cabin was not pressurized, I'd need oxygen to fly above 12,500 feet. I would have to fly higher than that to clear bad weather conditions, which meant refilling the oxygen tank along the way. Unfortunately, oxygen was not readily available outside the U.S.

The biggest drawback was that the Piper Saratoga was a piston-engine airplane and used avgas (aviation gasoline). A lot of airports in Asian countries did not have avgas, including China and Russia.

These restrictions made plotting a route very difficult. If I could not fly through China and Russia, I might have to fly through Southeast Asia and northern Australia, then island hop across the Pacific to Hawaii. From Hawaii, I would need an extra fuel tank to fly to Los Angeles. That's 2,200 nautical miles and would have meant 14 hours nonstop.

The more I tried for a work-around, the clearer it became that I was going to have to get a different airplane. Another critical reason to make a change was that flying across China would have been out of the question in a Piper Saratoga.

How could the first Chinese citizen to fly around the world do it without going through China's airspace?

China's airspace is controlled by the military. The People's Liberation Army uses a system of seven regions: Shenyang, Beijing, Lanzhou, Jinan, Nanjing, Guangzhou, and Chengdu. To fly across China from Hong Kong to Russia requires permission from five regions. Flying into China is difficult, but easier than flying across it.

Another Big Hairy Audacious Goal I had my heart set on was landing at Beijing Capital International Airport. Private aviation, at the time, was nearly unknown in China, and no single-engine plane had landed at Beijing Capital International Airport since World War II. It was the second busiest airport in the world and the busiest airport in China.

By Civil Aviation Administration of China (CAAC) policy, any airport with more than 200 takeoffs and landings daily is classified as "busy," and single-engine airplanes are banned from using them. Flying into Beijing seemed like the most impossible part of my dream. Even though I was not sure if I could fly into China and land at Beijing, I still wanted to get my airplane and myself ready for the possibility of doing so.

By the end of 2010, I'd decided I needed a turbine-engine airplane burning Jet-A fuel. I researched single-engine turbine airplanes, including the Cessna Caravan, Quest Kodiak, Piper Meridian, Piper Jetprop, Socata TBM, Pilatus.

I wanted an airplane with a pressurized cabin. To go above bad weather, I would have to fly higher than 12,500 feet. Oxygen was not readily available in most Asian airports. So I ruled out the Cessna Caravan and Quest Kodiak.

Piper Meridian and JetProp were very similar airplanes, one was completed in the factory and the other was a turbine engine conversion from Piper Malibu and Mirage. I preferred the factory made Piper Meridian.

When I compared three factory-made turbo-props with pressurized cabins: Piper Meridian, Socata TBM, and Pilatus PC-12, it was clear that Socata TBM was an excellent airplane for this trip. It was the fastest of the three. Its range was 1,500 nautical miles at Long Range Cruise, much farther than Piper Meridian's 1,000 NM. TBM's payload with maximum fuel was 800 lbs, greater than Piper Meridian's capacity. I eliminated Piper Meridian and focused on Socata TBM and Pilatus PC-12

Both were great airplanes for the trip. Pilatus PC-12 offered the longest range and biggest payload among single-engine turbo-prop airplanes. It could carry nine passengers and cruise 1,500 NM. Or it could fly with no passenger and cruise 2,200 NM. It is a very capable and flexible airplane. However, I didn't expect to carry a lot of passengers and a 1,200 NM range was adequate for my planned stops. The Socata TBM was not only faster but also $1 million cheaper than the Pilatus PC-12. I decided on that plane for the mission.

The best time to complete this trip was in summer. Winter over the Bering Sea and Greenland would have been too icy for the small airplane. The window of opportunity was to depart in May and finish in July.

I made the decision to change my airplane in December 2010 and the departure date was in May 2011. I had less than five months to complete preparations. Through extensive research, I located a low-time TBM700, serial number 30, and entered a purchase agreement on January 13, 2011. However, when a mechanic did a pre-purchase inspection, an FOD (Foreign Object Damage) issue was found in the turbine engine. That meant it had to be taken off the airplane and sent to Dallas Automotive hot section for repair. We didn't close the transaction until March 2011. I finally went to Minneapolis to pick up the airplane with copilot Don Davis on March 16, 2011. Now I had about 60 days left to get fully trained in this much faster and much more complex airplane.

I attended one week of training at SIMCOM Training Center in Orlando, Florida, and practiced as many emergency procedures as possible, including engine failure, fire in the cockpit, landing gear failure, among others. Next, I took many trips with my family and friends and visited remote places. I had never flown from Memphis to the Bahamas at 28,000 feet in three and a half hours. With the Socata TBM, it was not only possible but easy. I loved this airplane!

I loved it so much, that I reserved a unique registration: N168CW. "N" is the country code for the U.S. and "CW" means Chen Wei. In Chinese, the last name is spoken first, and people call me "Chen Wei" instead of "Wei Chen." The number "168" is lucky in China and means "plain sailing leads to success." I needed all the blessings I could get.

Despite the plane's advantages, the change presented a huge challenge. Turbine-engine airplanes are built for more experienced pilots, someone with 1,000-plus hours of flying experience, because it flies much faster and higher than piston-engine planes. Insurance requirements are significantly greater for a pilot with relatively little flying time, let alone someone who wanted to fly the plane around the world. Getting insurance for the entire trip was another hurdle, as European countries required $7 million in liability insurance and Hong Kong required $15 million to allow me to land. Finding an insurance company to underwrite a rookie pilot for the most challenging trip was not easy. I secured the necessary insurance two weeks before departure and scratched off another "small" task on my must-have list.

Realizing the risk, I wanted to make sure my family and business would be well taken care of in case of any tragedy. I consulted with my personal lawyer to put everything in place: life insurance, will, and succession plans. I couldn't eliminate the emotional loss of my family, but at least I didn't want them to bear a financial burden. Making these arrangements led me to appreciate my life a lot more and understand how blessed I was to be loved by so many great family members and friends.

Just days before my target date, I had a cross-country flight. The weather was perfect and air traffic was light. There was not much communication with air traffic control (ATC). In a cloudless blue sky, I said to myself, "How much would someone have to pay me not to fly this trip?"

I started thinking how much the adventure was worth to me. The opportunity to become the first Chinese citizen to fly a single-engine airplane around the world; the opportunity to promote general aviation in China, which was in its infancy; the opportunity to fly into Chinese airspace and possibly land in Beijing; the opportunity to raise money and awareness for St. Jude from contributors worldwide; the opportunity to promote our beloved city of Memphis; the generous support from the Chinese government, which sent a performance troupe to cities along the route; and the opportunity to celebrate with members of Chinese communities around the world.

How much was that worth to me?

More importantly were the unconditional support from my mom and dad and from my lovely wife Isabel who'd said, "Yes," and was willing to take the biggest risk of her life in supporting my dream. It was she who would bear the consequence of tragedy.

How much was it worth?

As I considered these things, I realized there was not enough money in the world to take away this dream from me.

Then came departure day and that early morning call. All I could think of as I listened to Thierry's news of the volcanic eruption in Iceland, was that I couldn't start the journey. All of the effort in the past 18 months, could be suffocated in clouds of ash. The effects of the eruption on aviation were unknown, and I couldn't wait even two weeks to depart because my visas were date specific. If I missed an entry date, I would not have time to get another visa en route. I realized I might have to give up this trip for a full year.

"Damn that volcano."

FLIGHT LOG: MEMPHIS TO PARIS

MAY 22, 2011—JUNE 3, 2011

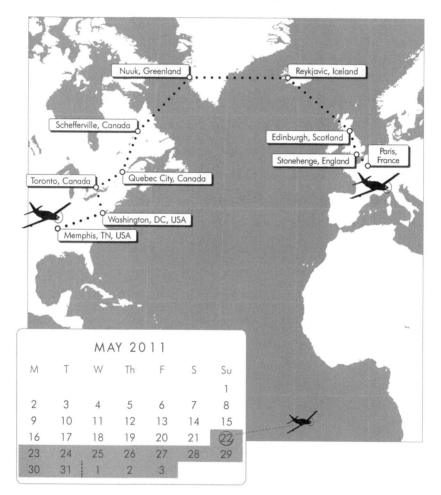

CHAPTER TWO

VOLCANIC ASH
(MEMPHIS TO PARIS)

What kind of man would live where there is no danger?
I don't believe in taking foolish chances. But nothing can
be accomplished by not taking a chance at all.

- Charles Lindbergh

I spent the morning on the phone discussing flight alternatives with aviation friends. Two ideas came up. One was to fly westward to Canada, Alaska and Russia, instead of the planned eastbound route to Greenland, Iceland, Europe. The first around the world trip in 1924 was in that direction, but I quickly realized I couldn't because of my visa dates. I needed to arrive in Russia in July, not in May.

Another idea was to add a bladder tank for extra fuel that would increase the airplane's range. That way I could fly straight from Canada to Europe without stopping in Greenland or Iceland. There wasn't time for that. We'd need approval from the Federal Aviation Administration (FAA), and there were engineering problems. It would have taken at least two weeks.

After learning about the volcanic eruption in Iceland, Isabel became concerned and asked, "Are you going to take off today?" I told her calmly I would evaluate the situation and decide later.

Finally, after five or six hours of struggling over the decision and weighing all options along with risks and rewards, I decided to begin the journey.

For one thing, it made more sense to get closer to the volcano than to wait in Memphis. If the conditions changed, I'd be in a better position to grab a window of opportunity, if I were closer to Iceland. If I had to wait two or three weeks, I'd rather be in Canada than Memphis.

I realized that if I had this Big Hairy Audacious Goal, I couldn't give it up just because of an unexpected difficulty, not even a huge volcanic eruption. I needed to keep advancing toward the goal, no matter how difficult. I recalled the 20 Mile March theory by Jim Collins and Morten T. Hansen in the book *Great by Choice*.

The 20 Mile March theory derives from the divergence in strategy between explorers Roald Amundsen and Robert Falcon Scott in their efforts to be the first to reach the South Pole in October 1911.

Amundsen adhered to a regimen of consistent progress, never going to the point of exhaustion in good weather, yet pressing ahead in nasty weather to stay on pace. Amundsen limited his well-tuned team to between 15 and 20 miles per day, in a relentless march to 90 degrees south.

In contrast, Scott would sometimes drive his team to its limit on good days and then remain in tents during bad weather. At one point Scott faced six days of gale-force winds and traveled on none, whereas Amundsen faced 15 and traveled on eight.

Amundsen reached the South Pole at his target pace, averaging 15.5 miles per day. Scott in contrast fell behind early, as worsening conditions were exacerbated by lack of preparation. He and two surviving team members died 11 miles short of a supply station on their return journey.

I realized that if I had this Big Hairy Audacious Goal, I couldn't give up.

Some delay might be unavoidable, but cancelling wasn't an option. I hadn't expected my around-the-world trip to be easy. This test just came a little earlier than I'd anticipated, and it was a small part of what I'd have to overcome.

I talked it over with my pilot friend, Rob Williams, who had agreed to fly with me to Canada, and we finally took off at one o'clock in the afternoon on May 22, 2011, much later than I had planned. My family came to the airport and hugged me and wished me good luck. Isabel asked me about the volcano again. I assured her that I would not take any unnecessary risk. She smiled, buoying me with her confidence.

Memphis was enveloped by thunderstorm, but we flew through it. The first stop was Washington, D.C., where more than 150 Chinese people waited in the airport and congratulated me for attempting this mission. They even organized a children's dance performance in the hangar to celebrate the first leg of the journey.

Just weeks earlier, on May 4, 2011, we flew to Washington D.C. for a news conference at the National Press Club. Counsel General, Chen Xiongfeng, came and made speech about the significance of the trip. I also met Chen Xiangmei, the wife of Lieutenant General Claire Lee Chennault, an aviation hero famous for his leadership of the "Flying Tigers" and Chinese Air Force in World War II. At the age of 86, she seldom came out to meet anyone. Because of her love of aviation, she was excited about this trip and wrote "Happy Flying, Happy Life forever!" in a personal message to me. The next day, we flew to Toronto, Canada. More than 50 Chinese people came to the airport and reporters from CCTV came to interview me. The interview was broadcast across China, making my flight national news. The local Chinese community also hosted a warm reception for me.

In Toronto, I had nothing to do but monitor conditions following the volcanic eruption. Things didn't look promising. Thick ash clouds hovered over Greenland and Iceland, right in the middle of my route. I could do nothing but wait, as the danger posed by ash trumped all other considerations. Iceland and Greenland are so far north that if the engine failed, I'd have nowhere to land. The chance of survival would be essentially zero. It was a risk of death that I wasn't willing to take. I was stranded in northeastern Canada, as the Memphis newspaper, *The Commercial Appeal*, reported.

On May 25, 2011, the volcano stopped erupting. It no longer was blow out clouds of ash, but existing ash rose as high as 50,000 or 60,000 feet. My cruising altitude was FL270, or 27,000 feet, so I'd be flying through the thick of it. Not even a big commercial airliner could go above it, and certainly not a single-engine airplane like mine. At least the situation was not getting worse. With this encouraging news, I flew from Toronto to Quebec City, Canada, on May 25, 2011. I had advanced nearer to Iceland and got a closer look at the ash.

A Chinese friend of mine, Jason Zhang, was living in New York at the time. He is a passionate private pilot. When I told him about my plans to fly around the world in early 2011, he immediately said he wanted to be part of it. He asked me if he could fly with me from Quebec City to Paris, knowing this was the most dangerous route of the entire trip. I agreed. Of course, he hadn't expected a volcano eruption in Iceland. Even with that event, however, he joined me in Quebec City on May 26. We met in the historic hotel Fairmont Le Chateau Frontenac and hugged each other warmly. The excitement of being part of my around-the-world trip must have outweighed the risk of losing his life.

On May 27, 2011, the ash appeared to be abating, as it moved higher and drifted toward the North Pole. We flew from Quebec City to Schefferville, Canada, for a fuel stop. This is a town with only 213 people. This isolated spot is disconnected from any road network and accessible only by airplane or train. Most people have never heard of it, but it was a vital fuel stop that would enable us to fly to Nuuk, Greenland. After we fueled the airplane, it was well past noon. There was nothing in Schefferville Airport; no hotel, no food, no one but the guy who handled fuel.

We were the closest to the volcano and its ash as we'd ever been. I was about to meet the source of my worries. We could not afford any mistake during the flight, from Schefferville, Canada, to Nuuk, Greenland. This was the leg in which we were most likely to encounter ash. This was the leg for which we had no rescue plan or option. We'd be over either mountains of ice or a frozen sea from Canada to Greenland. On this leg, mechanical failure meant death!

We were monitoring the U.K.'s National Weather Service, the Met Office, and its London Volcanic Ash Advisory Center (VAAC) hourly. The VAAC provided reports and forecasts on the movement of volcanic ash plumes covering Iceland and the northeastern part of the North Atlantic Ocean. We learned that the ash had moved above 40,000 feet, well above our flight level of 27,000 feet. It had also moved northwest toward to the North Pole, north of our intended route. Everything looked better.

I was surprised at how quickly the volcano stopped erupting and the ash had dissipated, unlike the Eyjafjallajökull volcano eruption in April 2010 that lasted more than one month. The Grímsvötn eruption, although much larger than the Eyjafjallajökull eruption, lasted less than four days. I felt that there was someone praying for me and that God indeed was my co-pilot.

However, in the morning of May 27, 2011, the Greenlandic airspace was still closed due to high concentrations of ash over Greenland and the North Atlantic. That day, Air Greenland cancelled most of its flights; more than 1,000 passengers and 20 tons of cargo were affected. Greenland's west coast – from Nuuk northward was covered in varying concentrations of ash. According to an Air Greenland official news release, it was expected the airline would be able to fly in the south and from Narsarsuaq to Nuuk by afternoon West Greenland time.

The Greenlandic airspace was open for local private flights only. Even though Air Greenland commercial flights to Nuuk were cancelled, we felt confident about flying into Nuuk after carefully studying the VAAC volcano ash chart. We decided to continue our flight at two in the afternoon.

The first thing we did was put on our "Gumby suits," worn only in emergency conditions, in case we had to crash land. The suit is made of red, fire-retardant neoprene for high visibility on the open ocean. Neoprene is a synthetic rubber with closed-cell foam, which contains a multitude of tiny air bubbles, making the suit a flotation device. In case of a crash landing, we could float easily in the ocean, waiting for a rescue team. However, in freezing water, we could last no more than 30 minutes to one hour. The survival suit would also help protect us from burns by fuel. Those were far better odds then we would have had in our normal flight clothes, but still very slim.

The suit is heavy and bulky, making the person wearing one look like Gumby, the children's TV character. We had to help each other get into them. After all the work putting on the suit, the next challenge was getting into the cockpit. Access to the cockpit of a small airplane is tight already. And with the survival suit, I was 30 percent fatter!

After squeezing into the plane, I turned on tracking instruments, including a handheld Personal Locator Beacon (PLB) and the on-board flight-tracking device. The airplane was equipped with emergency locator transmitters (ELTs). In case of a crash landing, the ELTs would deploy automatically and transmit a distress signal for rescue teams.

For an extra lifeline, I purchased a live on-board flight-tracker from Spidertracks. The device sends the GPS location of the airplane in real-time every minute to Spidertracks servers, which store the airplane's location in real time. It is equipped with an SOS function. If the system loses contact with the airplane, an SOS would be sent automatically. More importantly, Spidertracks uses the Iridium satellite network, which ensures that the device works everywhere in the world, even in a remote area of Greenland. If we crashed in an area where ELT signals could not be received, the GPS location from Spidertracks could provide the plane's location to the last minute.

If we had to ditch in the ocean, the airplane may sink, leaving us floating in the open sea. Therefore, I carried a Personal Locator Beacon (PLB). The PLB transmits distress signals on 406 MHz, an internationally recognized distress frequency, to COSPAS-SAR-SAT, an International Satellite System for Search and Rescue. Each PLB is equipped with a unique 15-digit alphanumeric identifying code. This code is transmitted in electronic bursts to satellites and is linked to a computer database maintained by the National Oceanic and Atmospheric Administration.

After we took off from Schefferville, I was nervous but extremely focused. As we flew closer to Nuuk the sky became darker and darker. I was not sure whether it was because of the time or because of volcanic ash. I monitored the engine instruments closely even as I searched for any flat place to land in case of emergency. There was no place to land. There was only icy terrain or iceberg-riddled ocean. We flew in a dark sky above and ahead, but we were clear of volcanic ash, as we planned.

The flight from Schefferville to Nuuk was the longest 688 nautical miles I had ever flown. After two and a half hours, we landed at Nuuk Airport in the late evening on May 27, 2011.

Nuuk Airport was built on a leveled slope at the foot of Ukkusissat Mountain. The runway was elevated to compensate for a scarp immediately to the west of the airport. From northbound, we entered the downwind leg of the pattern, performed a full U-turn, flying directly over the city, and landed on a 3,100-foot STOL runway. We frequently encountered heavy turbulence during this approach but were lucky to have only slight turbulence during the landing. The view was astonishing during the approach, with the ocean on our left and icy mountains on our right. The relief of landing safely, however, overwhelmed that grand view!

Nuuk is the capital of Greenland. With 16,000 people, it is the smallest capital city in the world. I experienced nearly 24 hours of daylight for the first time. There was still light when I went to bed at midnight.

The next morning, we took our time studying the ash situation. We had cleared the first ash-threatened leg, but we were now closer to the source, the Grímsvötn volcano. While an ash cloud still menaced the atmosphere, it was well above our flight altitude of 27,000 feet.

Greenland is three times the size of Texas, with a total population of only 60,000 people, living in coastal cities. The Greenland ice sheet is vast, covering 660,235 square miles, roughly 80 percent of the world's largest island. The ice has a mean altitude of 7,005 feet, but reaches as high as 10,794 feet. Although we became less concerned about the volcanic ash, the flight from Nuuk, Greenland to Reykjavik, Iceland, was still the most dangerous route in the most remote area. We had to fly from the west coast of Greenland, crossing the ice sheet and Atlantic Ocean. The distance was 780 nautical miles and would take almost three hours, with two hours over ice and one hour over ocean.

Again, we put on our Gumby suits and turned on all tracking devices. Around noon we took off in a blue sky into a tail wind. We had no communication with any ATC for more than one hour over the Greenland ice sheet, and we were given only three frequencies to report our location after we crossed it.

We saw no sign of ash. All the worry since I left Memphis was gone. I couldn't have been in a better mood. I turned on the CD in the cockpit and played my favorite Chinese song, "Flying Higher" by Wang Feng. I sang along with it, even though only I could hear it. The real happy journey began.

As soon as we landed at Reykjavik in the afternoon of May 28, 2011, I went to the Blue Lagoon Geothermal Spa. In the land of fire and ice, a good hot soak was exactly what I needed to ease the pressures of the past week.

The next day, we flew from Reykjavik to Edinburgh, Scotland, officially crossing the Atlantic Ocean. Whoever says Scotland is a windy place isn't lying. We had crosswinds of more than 200 knots (230 miles per hour) at the flight level of 27,000 feet and about a 50-knot (57-mile per hour) wind during landing. Compared with risks of volcanic ash, these winds didn't concern me much. They actually made me happy, as I believed it was Scotland's strong winds that had pushed the volcanic ash toward the North Pole. Thank you, Scotland!

We arrived in Paris on May 31, 2011, on my 40th birthday.

After flying five consecutive days from Quebec City to Paris, I appreciated what Charles Lindbergh had accomplished in the early days of aviation, as the first person to fly solo across the Atlantic Ocean. On May 20, 1927, Lindbergh took off in The Spirit of St. Louis and flew from New York nonstop to Paris, a distance of nearly 3,600 statute miles, in 33.5 hours without the aid of an autopilot or GPS. Lindbergh faced many challenges, including storm clouds, wave tops, icing, flying blind though fog, navigating by the stars, and "dead reckoning." His historic flight embodies the central question: "What would you attempt to do if you knew you couldn't fail?"

From the moment Charles Lindbergh landed at Le Bourget Field in Paris at 10:22 pm on May 21, 1927, he achieved lifelong world fame. More importantly, he and his flight boosted the aviation industry. Over the remainder of 1927, applications for pilot's licenses in the U.S. tripled and the number of licensed aircraft quadrupled. The number of U.S. airline passengers increased by 3,000 percent, from 5,782 in 1926 to 173,405 in 1929. As Elinor Smith Sullivan, winner of the Best Woman Aviator of the Year Award in 1930, said, "It is hard to describe the impact Lindbergh had on people. Even the first walk on the moon doesn't come close."

My flight across the Atlantic Ocean started on almost the same day, 84 years later. It took Lindbergh 33.5 hours to cross the Atlantic Ocean, it took me five days. (He didn't have to deal with volcanic ash in Iceland!) I knew that my flight would not have an impact close to that of Lindbergh. My hope was to promote Chinese aviation and show 1.3 billion people what private flying was about and that a Chinese citizen could fly around the world in a single-engine airplane.

I celebrated my fortieth birthday alone by sleeping more than 12 hours straight. After flying five consecutive days across the Atlantic Ocean and fearing for my life, I was exhausted, both mentally and physically. I took a three-day break in Paris, not to see the city, which I'd visited many times, but to catch my breath and prepare for the next leg of the journey.

MEMPHIS TO PARIS

From top to bottom: Volcanic ash in and around Iceland;
Greenland; fortieth birthday celebration in Paris

FLIGHT LOG: PARIS TO DUBAI

JUNE 3, 2011—JUNE 23, 2011

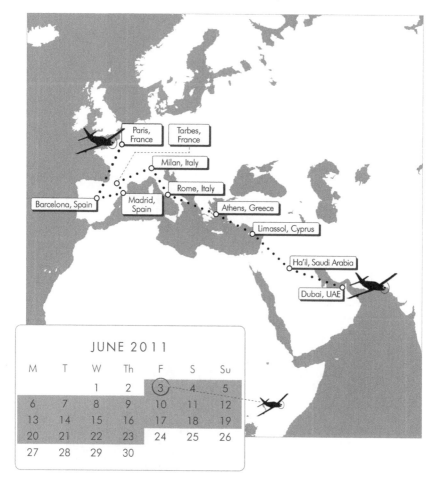

CHAPTER THREE

AMERICAN DREAM
(PARIS TO DUBAI)

Dreamers. Thinkers. Doers.
- Slogan for the University of Memphis

n June 3, 2011, I flew from Paris to Madrid. From the moment I landed, the local Chinese community embraced me, big time!

A group of 17 performers sent from China and sponsored by the central government put on a show to celebrate this historic trip. The theme was "Embrace China, Happy Flying." The troupe of singers, dancers, and acrobats had performed at receptions in Madrid, Barcelona, and Rome. The sense of national pride I saw among my fellow Chinese across the world was both humbling and inspiring. This flight meant nearly as much to many of them as it did to me.

Members of the local Chinese community picked me up at the airport and took me to dinner. We dined with a few hundred other community members. Across a Chinese-style roundtable from me was a man about 30 years old, who kept staring at me. He didn't say anything; he just kept looking at me with a respectful expression.

After dinner, he quietly introduced himself as Simon Bai. To my surprise, he spoke in the dialect of my hometown; we were from the same city, Changsha, Hunan. In China, the standard language is Mandarin but every town and city has its own dialect, and they're all quite distinct from each other. When Simon spoke authentic Changshanese, we were connected. That brought us close immediately, despite the fact that I lived in the U.S. and he was in Madrid. We started comparing notes and swapping stories about our hometown.

Later, I learned he's an entrepreneur who came to Madrid, got an education, and started a logistics business a few years ago. The business became successful, with headquarters in Madrid and branches in Italy and France. His story was very similar to mine. It made me think about my journey to the U.S. pursuing the "American Dream."

—

I came to Memphis in August 1996, thanks to a full scholarship from the International MBA program at the University of Memphis. Out-of-state tuition for foreign students pursuing an MBA was about $15,000 to $30,000 per year. Certainly no ordinary Chinese family could afford it. With the scholarship, the school waived my tuition. In addition, I received a monthly stipend of $250, which covered half my living expenses. To make up the other half, I worked as a delivery boy for the florist in the day and for Chinese restaurants in the evening and as a receptionist in the University's computer lab from midnight to the next morning.

The International MBA program offered different language tracks. Foreign students would be in the English track. American students could select a language. The program would find an internship for each student in the country of the selected language. In the case of Spanish, for example, the program would find an internship in Mexico, Spain, or another country where Spanish is the official language. For us in the English track, the program would find an internship at a U.S. company based in Memphis. This was a great opportunity for foreign students. Not only could we make money as interns, we gained experience in a U.S. company, which was essential for our careers.

I worked in the marketing department of Sedgwick Noble Lowndes, a benefits consulting firm, for six months. Emersion in the corporate environment of an American company was quite a learning experience. I enjoyed the spacious working cubicle, friendly co-workers, and state-of-the-art facility. However, the nine-to-five pace was too slow. I was paid $12 per hour, $2,500 per month, the most money I've ever made working for someone else. But I couldn't find my passion in this job.

When I graduated in August 1998, I faced the toughest decision in my life. At that point, the U.S. economy was relatively good. There were plenty of jobs available, even for foreigners with MBAs fresh out of school. All of my classmates found good jobs. As foreign students, we were very limited to what we could do. We came here under F-1 student visas. After graduation, we had to find corporate sponsors for H1-B working visas. Otherwise, we had to return to our homeland, so finding a job seemed the only choice for me.

Like my classmates, I spent a lot of time preparing my professional resume with the help of many people to perfect it. It was one page, had a clear structure and was accurately worded, with a concise list of skills. I even fretted over what fonts to use to make it more attractive. But I couldn't put my passion into this one-page document.

I've got a lot of passion! My passion was to do something that could leverage my knowledge of China along with the knowledge I'd acquired about the U.S.

Isabel and I got married right before I graduated. She was still a PhD student at the University of Memphis majoring in Biomedical Engineering with three years left. When I told her that I wanted to start my own company, she said, "Ok." She didn't even ask "Why?" or "How?"

I knew "Why" but I didn't know "How?" I had been an MBA student for two years, so my English was adequate. However, I had no social network in business, as most of my friends were still in school. I had no business plans or ideas, or partners, or investors. Worst of all, I had no money.

So how did I start a company with no funds? Luckily, credit was loose. I had always paid my bills on time and kept a very good credit history. Even as a poor student, I was able to get four to five credit cards. Each credit card had about a $10,000 credit limit. The credit card companies offered zero percent interest for six or

12 months to lure customers, so I could run up a debt and then transfer the money to another card to pay it off without incurring interest charges. The credit card companies were my investors, but I was glad they didn't ask for any equity in my company.

Now that I had "money," the next thing to do was to formalize the company: Sunshine International Corp. I registered the company, rented a 200-square-foot office at $300 per month and installed a phone and a fax. Then I spent $700 on office furniture that John Chen helped me assemble. I did all this with credit card debt. I titled myself "Chief Executive Officer" and made my own business card using my printer at home. Officially, I was in business.

Having an office kept me focused. I wasn't dabbling. I took my startup very seriously. My overhead was $600 per month, which was not a lot of money, but it was more than my monthly living expenses at that time, which also were covered by credit card debt.

But, without a business plan, what should I do?

I went to the office every day at 8 am and came home at 5:30 pm, even though I was the only employee. My two Bibles were the Yellow Pages and the Chambers' Directory. I wish we'd had Google at the time. Every day, I'd go through the Yellow Pages and the Chambers' Directory to find companies, then call and introduce myself. Without a social network, my only connection to the business world was the phone line.

I did this every day for three months and contacted all kinds of businesses. I created a list of potential customers and called every single one of them. Whenever they had a slight interest in talking to me, I asked for appointments. I would put in 120 percent effort if they gave me the slightest chance. I worked on apparels, industrial gloves, feed additives, automobile parts, casting products, forging products, plastic products, industrial tools, tires, glasses, industrial nails, and many other products.

In *Great by Choice*, Jim Collins and Morten T. Hansen write about how successful companies "Fire Bullets, then Cannonballs." This theory derives from a strategic encounter between two battleships. In the old days of sea warfare, when a battleship came after you, you could fire all the bullets you had, but they wouldn't sink the ship. If you fired cannonballs from the start, you would likely miss your target and waste ammunition. Shooting bullets could help you calibrate the curve and enable to properly aim your cannons. Once you've done that, you need to load the cannonballs and take down the battleship.

In October 1998, two months after I started the company, I met a local customer who asked me: "Wei, are you able to import scaffolds?" Well, I didn't know what a scaffold was. Two years of International MBA study never taught me how to spell "scaffold." But I said, "Sure, let me try." Starting with scaffolding products was just like starting with any other product. They were my "bullets" so to speak, but I quickly realized the potential of these products.

In 1999, very few companies were importing scaffolding because of quality concerns. Not a single factory in China could manufacture scaffolds to meet U.S. standards. Most places in China still used bamboo. U.S. customers didn't want to risk their worker's lives by purchasing sub-standard scaffolds from China. The risk of a lawsuit outweighed any economic benefits, even though the products could be manufactured much cheaper in China.

In Chinese, "危机" means "danger and opportunity." When others saw the danger, I saw the opportunity. I brought American quality standards back to the Chinese factories and taught them on how to improve their products. This was easier than I expected, as all of them were eager to learn. Another challenge was market perception. Most customers had no faith in the quality of Chinese scaffolds. It was a tremendous effort to educate customers one by one. To instill confidence, I purchased expensive Product Liability Insurance in the U.S. Once they understood I could ensure quality standards, sales became much easier.

In 1998, after four months in business, I had almost $10,000 in credit card debt. Early 1999, I made a large sale of $120,000 to a customer in New York and he trusted me and paid me $36,000 deposit, when I had no real operation. With this deposit, I paid off all my debt and sent the balance to the factory to manufacture the order. In 1999, I made close to $1 million in sales with more than a 40 percent margin, merely by trading directly with China. Initially, customers paid a 30 percent deposit when they placed an order, with the balance due when they received the products. Quality had to be good. After I received a deposit, I would negotiate payment terms with factories. I would pay a 30 percent deposit when I placed an order and the remaining balance upon delivery. After building relationships with factory owners and increasing their volumes, they allowed 30 days after delivery to receive the balance, so cash flow was positive. The more products I sold, the more cash I had available. I was ready to load all my energy and resources to focus on this product line and "fire the cannonballs."

After carefully analyzing the market, I decided to build a distribution network in the U.S. Not all customers could wait 10 weeks for delivery. Having inventory on the ground could bring more value to customers and serve a broader base.

I started with a branch in New York in 2000, the largest potential market in the U.S. That was the most difficult time in my start-up. Due to a lack of knowledge, I had catastrophic quality problems when I found the entire initial inventory didn't match products in the market. Customers couldn't use our products with their existing inventories. It almost killed the business when I was stuck with non-compatible inventory. I had to offer significant discounts below cost to get rid of the "bad" inventory.

After I had built up the "right" inventory, the New York branch became an instant success, largely because competition was scarce. Six months after I opened the branch, I hired Tom Thayavally and empowered him to run it like it was his own. From day one until now, 13 years later, he has been the best branch manager. New York has been the top-performing branch for 10 consecutive years. Tom has grown the business to $5 million with only seven employees. The best part for me has been that I only have to visit his branch once a year. I spend my time on continuing to build a national distribution network.

We opened distribution centers in Houston in 2001, Los Angeles in 2002, Atlanta in 2003, and finally in Memphis in 2005. I would stay in each city for six months to open the branch. Instead of renting warehouses, we bought them. It showed our commitment to the marketplace and our long-term plan. We were here to stay and serve our customers. None of our competitors had the kind of distribution network we did. Within six years, we became one of the leading players in the market. We had triple-digit growth in the early years and averaged more than 40 percent growth in 10 consecutive years. We even made it to the list of fastest growing companies in the U.S. ranked by *Inc.* Magazine.

As our business grew rapidly, purchases from our vendors in China became a bottleneck. Our customers demanded consistently high quality products, and we could only control our vendors so much. More and more competitors came into the market by importing scaffolds from various factories. To further differentiate ourselves and bring more value to our customers, we decided to build our own factories, a huge undertaking given my lack of manufacturing know-how.

Our next move, or "cannonball," was to build an "American factory on Chinese land." Through research, I found the most favorable city was Chenzhou, Hunan. It was in my home province where relationships were easier to build, and it was close to the port of Shenzhen in Hunan province. Because I built a relationship with Chinese government officials and we were providing employment opportunities and tax benefits to the city, we were able to ask them to build the factory for us. The speed and efficiency of this Chinese government project was unreal. We signed the contract in May 2004, and less than eight months from the day they had built a 100,000-square-foot manufacturing facility with a dorm, kitchen, and office space on 250,000 square feet of farmland, that was basically a mud flat. We were in full production by 2005. The quality became more consistent and the supply more reliable. We were able to develop new products. The factory was operating at full capacity within one year. We opened a second factory near Shanghai in 2006. These "cannonballs" were flying full speed.

———

Simon and I developed a close friendship very quickly, thanks to our hometown connection and the incredible kindness and hospitality both he and his wife showed me in the two days I was in Madrid. As I planned for the next leg, from Madrid to Barcelona, the thought of leaving them behind was difficult.

The night before my departure, Simon asked whether he could join me for a part of the trip. I was surprised by his request since he had never flown in a small plane. For non-pilots, the perceived risk of a small airplane is normally very high. After having known me for only two days, the kind of trust he placed in me was amazing. I was not sure about his request and asked him, "Why."

He said this was a once-in-a-lifetime opportunity to be part of something not only inspiring, but something that would enter the historical record. How likely was it such an opportunity would come again? He was willing to risk the unknown and put his life in my hands.

It wasn't until much later that he told me his family was not in favor of his going and had given him a lot of grief over that decision. He had a baby, about a year old, and his family had no knowledge of small airplanes. They couldn't understand why he'd want to do something that they saw as life-endangering. His decision to join me despite his family's opposition was for him truly a leap of faith.

On June 6, 2011, we flew to Barcelona, Spain. A newly wedded couple, Lawson and Cynthia Baker, from Memphis arrived the same day at the start of their honeymoon. Lawson's father, Jim Baker, is a close friend and was a big supporter of the St. Jude Fundraiser Gala that kicked off my flight. When he found out his son's honeymoon matched my trip schedule, he asked whether they could join a portion to celebrate their honeymoon. I was very happy to do that and flew them to France and Italy. What a special wedding gift!

The airplane had a problem with the inertia separator, a device that protects the engine from FOD damage. It was stuck open and I couldn't close it. The airplane lost 20% engine performance at high altitude. Two maintenances shops in Madrid and Barcelona worked on it but couldn't fix it. To repair it, we flew to the airplane's factory in Tarbes, France, on June 8. It was very lucky that I discovered this problem near the factory and was able to get it fixed without delaying the journey.

We spent 10 days together from Madrid to Barcelona, Tarbes, Milan, and Rome. At that point, Simon left me and went back to Spain. I continued my flight to Athens, Greece on June 12, 2011, then to Limassol, Cyprus on June 14, 2011.

The journey from Paris to Limassol was the most enjoyable part of the whole trip. The flying was easy, just like flying in the U.S., the weather was pleasant, and the cities were interesting. I traveled these cities with my new friend from my hometown, and we had a lot of fun together. At each stop along the way, we received a grand reception at the airport.

On June 16, 2011, I planned to fly from Limassol, Cyprus, to Dubai, UAE, with a fuel stop in Saudi Arabia. Originally I planned to stop in Cairo, Egypt, and visit the pyramids. The unrest of the Arab Spring movement that had begun in April in Egypt made that unwise, so I canceled my stop in Cairo and flew over it. I had hoped to visit Israel as well, but if my passport had Israel's stamp in it, I wouldn't be able to go other countries in the Middle East.

Once I left Cypress, private flying became much more complicated in terms of flight permits and local handling. The U.S. and most European countries support private planes, and getting flying permits is easy. However, private planes are very rare in the Middle East, India, Asia, and Russia, and this greatly changed my flying during the second half of the trip.

I couldn't fly direct from Cyprus to Dubai because I had to avoid Iraq and Kuwait. So I detoured. From Cypress, I went southwest toward Egypt, then into Saudi Arabia. I didn't want to spend a night in Saudi Arabia and planned just a fuel stop at Riyadh, after which I'd head straight to Dubai. It was a total of eight hours of flying in one day.

Because of a strong head wind, I couldn't reach the scheduled fuel stop at Riyadh. Instead, I had to land in a small airport in Ha'il, Saudi Arabia. It was in the middle of nowhere, just desert, and the temperature was over 110 degrees when I landed. After I shut down my engine and opened the door, I saw no one except for a few soldiers with machine guns walking over to my airplane. I tried to talk to them, but they didn't understand English and I couldn't speak Arabic. We were stuck and didn't know what to do.

About 10 minutes later, a gentleman dressed in traditional Muslim clothes and headgear came over. He spoke English and asked whether we had a landing permit. I told him that we ran out the fuel and couldn't reach our intended destination. He agreed to sell us fuel, but I had to fill the tank myself. It was noon and the sun was blazing hot. I could smell Jet-A fumes as I fueled the airplane.

After that task, another problem arose: how could I pay for it? They told me they wouldn't take a check or a credit card. Clearly, I wasn't carrying any Saudi riyals. Finally, they agreed to accept U.S. dollars in the exact amount without change. I had carried more than $10,000 U.S. dollars with me, and it worked out well. I was thinking that most of Saudi Arabia's oil exports are priced in dollars anyway.

After I fueled the airplane and paid cash for the cheap fuel, I asked where the bathroom was. I had not been to the bathroom for six hours and wanted to go before my next long leg to Dubai. The translator told the soldiers my request. They hesitated as the only bathroom was in their dorm. However, they understood that I had no other choice. Finally one solider escorted me to it through their dorm.

I also asked if there was something we could get to eat since we haven't had anything for six hours, but there was nothing at the airport. They offered to escort me outside the airport to get something. I quickly said no, as I didn't want to leave my airplane unattended. Hungry, hot, and intimidated, we wanted to get out as soon as possible.

After the unpleasant fuel stop at Ha'il, Saudi Arabia, we flew another three hours and landed in Dubai in the evening.

COMING TO AMERICA

First arrival in America

First dorm in America

University of Memphis graduation photo

University of Memphis

ENTREPRENEURSHIP

First office

First container of scaffold

Winning executive of the year award

Performance group in Spain

Simon Bai's first flight to Barcelona

FLIGHT LOG: DUBAI TO AGRA

JUNE 3, 2011—JUNE 27, 2011

Dubai, UAE

Agra,
India

Muscat,
Oman

Ahmedabad, India

		JUNE 2011				
M	T	W	Th	F	S	Su
		1	2	3	4	5
6	7	8	9	10	11	12
13	14	15	16	17	18	19
20	21	22	23	24	25	26
27	28	29	30			

CHAPTER FOUR

PASSION FOR AVIATION
(DUBAI TO AGRA)

Without passion, you don't have energy. Without energy, you have nothing.
- Warren Buffett

In aviation, "error chain" refers to the concept that a series of events typically lead to an accident, rather than a single event. On the day I was flying into Agra, India, I had the most frightening flight of the whole trip, probably the most frightening time of my flying career. I was very lucky to survive the error chain.

On June 24, 2011, we planned to fly from Muscat, Oman, to Agra, India. The total distance was 1,088 nautical miles. I could fly nonstop for about four hours but had to land at Ahmedabad, India, to clear customs in order to continue the flight to Agra, India. It should have been an easy flight, but it turned out to be the scariest moment in my life.

We took off very early in the morning, considering that we would lose four hours due to the time difference. The flight from Muscat to Ahmedabad took about two and a half hours and we landed around 1 p.m. We had plenty of time before dark to finish the second leg from Ahmedabad to Agra, which was only 380 nautical miles, about an hour and a half flight.

Clearing customs, however, created a significant delay. We weren't able to depart until 4:30 p.m. That meant flying at night and landing at 7 p.m., after losing one hour due to the time difference.

I had planned the trip so I wouldn't fly at night. The risk of flying in a foreign country over unfamiliar terrain was too great. If we had been in the U.S. or Europe, I'd have waited until the next day. However, this was India. A delay would necessitate applying for a new flight permit, which could take days.

After weighing the pros and cons, we decided to go ahead and make the flight to Agra at night. After all, we were experienced in night flying. We departed at 4:45 p.m.

This was toward the end of June, the peak of monsoon season in India. Heavy rain clouds covered the sky. As soon as we took off, we were in clouds and flew under Instrument Meteorological Conditions (IMC). I didn't mind flying at night with a clear sky. However, flying through clouds at night over a foreign country was intimidating. "Well, it is a short flight and should be over soon," I told myself.

I was flying under instrument flight rules and monitoring the instruments closely. About 30 minutes from the destination, I saw the needle on the engine oil temperature gauge move above the red line. The prospect of losing the engine especially under these unfamiliar conditions scared the hell out of me.

Still, I didn't panic. I pulled the throttle back to 30 percent torque, hoping that would reduce the stress on the engine. My indicated air speed dropped from 180 knots to 120 knots, a hair above the white arc. I checked the engine oil pressure gauge, and it was normal. I removed my headphones and listened to the engine. I didn't hear anything abnormal. All other engine instruments: inter-stage turbine temperature, engine torque, high pressure rotor shaft speed (NG), and tachometer (RPM) were operating normally. That much was a relief. While we were only 20 minutes from the airport, I was extremely anxious to land.

As we neared the airport, Indian ATC cleared us to descend from 27,000 feet to 15,000 feet. The communication with Indian ATC was extremely difficult. We had trouble understanding the clearance from ATC due to the controllers' accents. I had to speak slowly and repeat myself a couple of times for them to understand.

At 15,000 feet, ATC transferred us to the next ATC and gave us a new frequency. When we switched the frequency and reported our position, we couldn't find anyone. We reported our position a few times, with no response. We lost the communication with ATC in the middle of all these problems.

We were desperate. We didn't want to deviate from the clearance and start to descend. I switched back to the old frequency and almost screamed at the previous ATC. "Wrong frequency! Request lower!" I made sure I spoke very slowly and clearly.

Finally, the ATC gave us another frequency, and I contacted the next ATC. When we were cleared to descend, we were only 10 nautical miles from the airport and still at 15,000 feet. Here is where my training came into play. I knew the capability of the Socata TBM well. I could pull the power back to idle and descend at 5,000 feet per minute, without damaging the airframe. A rapid descent in the clouds at night was frightening, but I had no time to think. I just acted. We still flew past the Agra airport and had to make a 180-degree turn.

As we were turning back, we asked for an ILS approach because we were still in IMC. ILS, or instrument landing system, is a ground-based instrument approach system that provides precision guidance to an aircraft that needs to land on a runway during IMC.

Now came the scariest moment: *ATC told us that ILS was not working in the Agra airport.*

I couldn't believe it. ILS was our lifeline in this situation. How could we find the runway and land properly if we didn't have ILS? If we couldn't land at Agra airport, then the alternative was to fly to New Delhi, about a half hour away. But how long could my single engine last with a potential engine oil temperature problem. We wanted to land as soon as possible. We were stuck, and couldn't decide whether to declare emergency or ask for the alternative airport at New Delhi. While we were thinking, we were flying at 200 knots, descending 5,000 feet per minute in the clouds at night, and banking 30 degrees back to the Agra airport

Things happened so fast that I didn't even have time to panic. My main focus was to fly the airplane. If I lost control due to a distraction, my error could be a link in a chain to disaster. Because

I was flying at night and in the clouds, I had to rely 100 percent on my instruments, not my body sense, to know what my airplane was doing. Without a visual reference, I was worried about hitting something, as I couldn't avoid high altitude obstacles. I hoped my engine wouldn't quit. I knew that if I declared an emergency, I would be grounded in India for a long time. This was the most dangerous period of our descent.

Here came our miracle.

When we descended to 2,500 feet, we came out of the clouds and the shining lights of Agra were right underneath us. We could see the ground and fly under visual flight rules. We were able to locate the Agra airport visually, using the onboard GPS as a reference. I was able to circle and land on the runway visually.

Getting out of monsoon season clouds at the last minute felt like I had a friend in the sky. Surviving the error chain was my best "Return on Luck." Return on Luck is another concept in Jim Collins and Morten T. Hansen's book *Great by Choice*. It is based on the notion that we all have luck events in our lives, and it is how we maximize them that makes us great.

—

The friend who joined me for this most frightening flight was a fellow YPO member, Samer Baassiri, from Dubai Chapter. In 2008, I joined the Young Presidents' Organization. The mission of YPO is to create better leaders through education and idea exchange. The organization has more than 21,000 members in more than 125 countries. It started in 1950 near New York City by Ray Hickok, who was 27 years old when he became the head of his family's 300-employee business.

He was overwhelmed, and in the interests of learning, he formed a circle of friends who were young corporate presidents. They began meeting regularly to share best practices and help one another both professionally and personally. Later this idea expanded into a worldwide organization. Membership is by invitation only, and it is prestigious to be asked to join. You have to have significant success in your business, either a family business or as an entrepreneur. Once you join, you are connected with members around the world. More importantly, you will join a forum with eight to twelve very close friends. Any issues you face, whether personal or professional, they provide a sounding board for good advice.

Before the trip, I emailed chairpersons of chapters in big cities on my route and told them about my trip and my reasons of doing it. I received warm receptions from many long-distance colleagues. Juan Del Yerro, a member of the Madrid chapter invited me to his home for dinner. In Barcelona, I was invited to an education event, at which Swami Parthasarathy at Vedanta Life Institute was the speaker. In Milan, I met Riccardo Lippolis, who is also a passionate pilot. He had planned to fly with us to Rome, but had to cancel due to his wife's illness. In Hong Kong, chapter chairman, Dave Boulanger, hosted a terrific dinner at the China Club attended by a few members to hear about this trip.

In Dubai, I made a life-long YPO friend.

Mr. Samer Baassiri heard about my flight and wanted to fly part of it as co-pilot. He is a private pilot, who has flown all over the world. He has a dream to become the first Lebanese to circumnavigate the world in a single engine airplane. He's a real adventurist, who traveled to more than 160 countries by the age of 38. To be qualified as a co-pilot on my airplane, he went to France for training in the Socata TBM prior to my arrival in Dubai.

Samer and I spent 10 days together, flying from Dubai to Oman, then to India, and Thailand. We didn't know each other and lived in different worlds, 8,000 miles apart. Our passion for aviation brought us together.

My love for aviation has brought me much fun and great friendships. But my road toward learning to fly has been bumpy.

I fell in love with the idea of flying as a child. In China when I was growing up, we didn't have toys. Even getting a kite was a financial challenge. My favorite game was to fold paper airplanes and compete with my friends to see whose would fly the farthest. We'd throw them from the balcony of our school. As I watched my airplane fly, I would daydream about what it would be like to really fly.

In the spring of 1988, I was an eleventh grade student at Mingde High School in Changsha, Hunan. The People's Liberation Army came to my high school to recruit air force pilots. There were military posters everywhere promoting the idea of being an air force pilot. They said that joining would make your family proud and it was a way to serve your country. I'd always dreamed of flying – now it looked like that might actually be possible.

I filled out an application and was already excited by imagining myself in the cockpit of an airplane. I went for the physical exam and did well. There were thousands of applicants for a handful of slots. Unfortunately, I wasn't drafted. I was heartbroken. They never told me why, but I've always suspected that it had something to do with my height. I was taller than average, and those chosen to be pilots were usually shorter. It seemed like the end of my dream to become a pilot. It wasn't until I came to the U.S. as a student that I got my first chance to fly.

My first roommate was a gentleman from Switzerland, Stephane Courtine. He had a German friend who was taking flying lessons for a private pilot's license in the States.

One day, Stephane said that his friend was going to take a cross-country trip to the Great Smokey Mountains and asked me if I wanted to fly with them. The cost was about $100.00. Even though that was a lot of money for me then, I didn't hesitate. I didn't even know there was such a thing as a private airplane until then. I was astonished.

We went to a small airport with a grass runway. It surprised me that an airplane could actually take off from a grass strip. We climbed into a four-seat Cessna 172, and Stephane was kind enough to let me sit in the co-pilot seat, knowing how eager and excited I was. Once airborne, the German pilot let me take over the yoke and fly the airplane. The feeling of freedom and flying like a bird exceeded my wildest imaginings.

When I got home, I called my parents in China to tell them about it. The international phone call cost $2 per minute then and I couldn't afford calling home every day and made the call only on the scheduled time over the weekend. But I couldn't wait that long. They couldn't conceive of the idea of a private airplane. How could such a thing be? It was as if I had told them I'd gone to the moon.

It was the '90s, and very few people in China had cars. I sent them the photos I'd taken from the trip, one of which I framed and hung on my wall.

Although I loved flying, I knew there was no way I could afford it on the $10 an hour salary I was making as a waiter. I was just scraping by as a student, and I couldn't see how it would ever be possible for me to afford the expenses involved with flying – the plane, the fuel, the license, the pilot training. I filed that one trip away as a happy memory, figuring that was my first and last experience in a small airplane.

I moved on, graduated, and started my company in 1998. I was so busy that I didn't have time to eat lunch for three years. A hobby was not something I could entertain, and piloting never entered my mind. However, a second chance to fly revived my dream.

In the spring of 2007, my friend John Dobbs Jr. and I were chatting about our travel plans. We found we would be in Atlanta at the same time and planned to return to Memphis on the same day. He said, "I'm going to fly back by myself. If you want to join me, you can come along." I already had a round trip ticket, but that was my last concern. I said immediately said, "Yes."

I met him at DeKalb-Peachtree Airport and got into his Cessna Citation. During that flight, I sat behind the cockpit and just watched, curious to see how he operated the airplane. He explained a few things to me, and it didn't seem too complicated. I asked him how he had learned to fly. He explained the process and shared his flying history. When we landed in Memphis, I went straight to the Air Venture Flight Center in the Olive Branch Airport and signed myself up for flight school.

I wanted to be a pilot!

By that time, my company was doing well. I could afford the $20,000 for a private pilot's license. Two days later, I was at the school to take a lesson. The first step was a half-hour "Discovery Flight" with the instructor to see if I liked it. I took it and I loved it. It was exactly what I wanted to do. Even though the application requirements for foreign pilot students became much harder after the 9/11 tragedy, it didn't discourage me. After a few weeks of a national security check, I enrolled in the program, bought all the material, and started learning how to fly.

After about one month of training and 10 hours of flying with the instructor, the next milestone was the First Solo Flight. The requirement was to execute three take-offs and landings in a pattern without the instructor on board. Even though I didn't feel I was ready, my instructor had the confidence that I could do it.

I had my first solo flight on July 8, 2007, a hot and humid day. The instructor flew the first take-off and landing with me. After we landed, she got off the airplane and I was on my own. She watched my flying closely from the taxiway and held a radio to communicate with me. The pressure of operating the airplane alone was nerve wracking. Knowing I had to land the airplane alone, I was extra cautious before takeoff. Unlike a car, you can't decide to quit before you complete the operation after you're airborne.

I went through the checklist a few times and made sure I didn't forget anything. Then I mentally walked through what I needed do at the each step: accelerating with directional control, pulling the nose off the ground at 65 knots, climbing at 80 knots, banking to turn to Crosswind, reaching the Pattern Altitude at Downwind and decreasing the power to 100-knot cruise speed, reducing power and lowering the flap to descend at the beam of runway end, turning to Base and verifying the descent rate, turning to Final Approach and keeping the speed at 90 knots, lining up the airplane with the Runway, flaring the airplane right before the reaching the ground, touching down at 70 knots and pulling the power to idle. On top of doing all that, I had to talk to the Airport Tower.

It all happened within two minutes but it seemed forever. Walking through it mentally before taking off helped a lot and I did three take-offs and landings successfully. The Air Traffic Controller was very accommodating when I made nervous mistakes during my communication. When I finished my third landing, he called on the radio: "Congratulation on your First Solo!"

As soon as I finished, my instructor ran to the airplane with scissors. She asked me to turn around and cut my shirttail. I was so happy, I didn't bother to ask why. Then she explained that, in American aviation lore, the removal of a new pilot's shirttail was a sign of the instructor's confidence after a student completes the first solo flight.

In the days of tandem trainers, the student sat in front, with the instructor behind. As there were often no radios in these early days, the instructor would tug on the student pilot's shirttail to get his attention, and then yell in his ear. A successful first solo flight was an indication that the student could fly without the instructor. Hence, there was no longer a need for the shirttail. She framed the shirttail for me.

I knew flying would become a part of my life. Even before I'd gotten my license, I started looking into buying an airplane. After three months of searching, I bought a 2001 Cessna 172 with 1,000 hours on October 10, 2007. I was able to finish the rest of my training and take my FAA Practical Test (check ride) in my own airplane.

It took me about six months to get my license. I officially became a pilot on November 10, 2007.

After earning a private license and buying an airplane, I wanted to fly everywhere. Then a pilot friend said something that brought me back to reality. He said, "Wei, congratulations on getting a license to kill yourself." This statement was blatant, but brutally true. I had a little over 50 hours and barely enough experience to fly an airplane in good weather. If I flew into bad weather or flew away from my home airport, my limited skills could put me in a dangerous situation that I might not be able to get out of.

I went back to flight school for more training. The next level was Instrument Rating. I signed up without hesitation. This training has improved my flying skills tremendously and given me the vital understanding of how to fly the airplane using instruments only.

After flying the Cessna 172 for two years, I wanted to fly faster and higher. On March 19, 2009, I bought my second airplane, a 2003 Piper Saratoga, a six-seat airplane that could cruise at 180 knots and fly at 20,000 feet. With this plane, I was able to take my family on vacations and make day trips for business to Atlanta, St. Louis, and Dallas among other cities. It made life much more convenient and saved me time. My dream had become a part of my life.

I always look for opportunities to fly different types of airplanes: aerobatic, warbirds, experimental, home-built, ultra-light, antique, military jets, and private jets. I wanted to know every airplane's performance, history, and flying capability. In the past four years, I have flown more than 20 kinds of airplanes. The experience of flying a new kind of airplane, learning it, mastering it, and loving it brought much joy to my life.

—

We were stranded in Agra for three days. We couldn't find any mechanics in India qualified to work on my Socata TBM, because there was no such airplane in India. I'd been communicating with the factory in France. People from there sent us many instructions and asked us to perform different tests. We did an engine ground run and couldn't find any problems. After multiple tests, we were convinced that the engine didn't have a problem and that the gauge was malfunctioning. We decided we could continue safely.

AVIATION

First airplane experience

First airplane experience

From top to bottom: first flight lesson; cutting the
shirttail after the first solo flight; getting licensed

Standing with Piper Saratoga

Cessna 172

With Chen Xiangmei, wife of Chinese aviation hero Lieutenant General
Claire Lee Chennault

祝福　陳瑋
快樂飛翔
永遠幸福
　　　陳香梅
2011年5月04日
於美京華盛頓

Chen Xiangmei's message:
"Happy Flying, Happy Life forever"

Oil temperature running hot

With Samer Baassiri

FLIGHT LOG: AGRA TO HONG KONG

JUNE 27, 2011—JULY 7, 2011

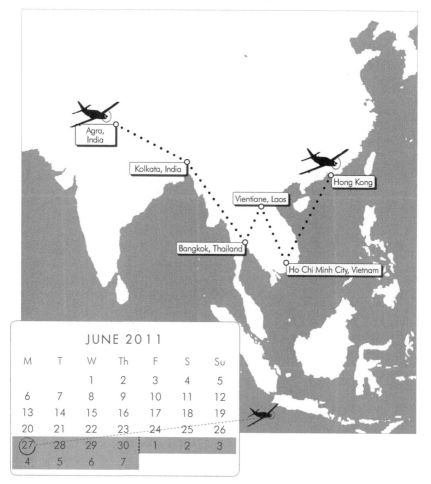

CHAPTER FIVE

CHINESE DREAM
(AGRA TO HONG KONG)

To get the full value of joy you must have someone to divide it with.

- Mark Twain

T he receptions we received across Europe, the Middle East and India were wonderful, but the one in Bangkok topped them all.

When my friend, Binling Wu, a community leader in Thailand, heard about the trip, he was excited that someone he knew was trying to make history. Before I began my journey, he asked me to stop in Bangkok. He promised he'd give me the grandest reception I'd ever seen – and he did.

On June 28, 2011, we flew from Kolkata, India, to Bangkok, Thailand. We took off later than planned and landed at about two in the afternoon. The director of the immigration office welcomed us to Thailand, and we were taken to the airport terminal in a private van. The airport workers unloaded our luggage, and we cleared customs in no time.

Ten to fifteen Chinese community leaders were waiting for us in the airport lounge. All of them wore suits and ties, despite the hot, humid weather of late June. They had been waiting for about three hours. I shook hands with each one as they took photos. Clearly, they felt pride in what I was trying to accomplish.

As they escorted me out of the reception lounge, we were met by more than 30 reporters. They were jostling with cameras and recorders and trying to interview me all at once. I stepped back as they pushed forward to get close to me, but guards helped me pass through. I was overwhelmed, but I quickly relaxed and answered their questions with a smile.

After the interviews, I was escorted out of the terminal where more than 300 people were lined up waving flags bearing my name in Chinese. Samer, who flew with me from India, asked, "What's going on?" I could only shake my head. I was as surprised as he was. We were there for about an hour, shaking hands and posing for pictures. Many brought Thai garlands made of fresh flowers and placed them around my neck. Of all the people I met, the most memorable was a 92-year-old grande dame who said with tears in her eyes, "Thank you for making Chinese people proud."

We were driven to the hotel in a vintage Rolls Royce. Upon arrival, we went straight to a banquet. We didn't even have time to check in. There were more than 1,000 people at the dinner. The Chinese ambassador to Thailand sat next to me. A stage was prepared with my picture in the center. It was a long dinner with many speeches from community leaders expressing excitement over the trip. I was tired but remained engaged in the conversations and activities.

The story ran on the front pages of Thai newspapers. I spent the next two days, from 6 a.m. to 9 p.m., attending receptions. I met thousands of Chinese people through different organizations. It was the first time I felt like a "celebrity." People wanted to have their pictures taken with me and asked for autographs. It took a lot of energy to satisfy the requests, but I didn't want to spoil this feeling and tried to connect with everyone I met.

Not in my wildest imagination did I expect the trip to have this kind of impact. Chinese people around the world were united in patriotism behind one man's adventure. What I saw in the reactions of my fellows convinced me that everything I'd done, every risk I'd taken had been worth it. People around me felt like they were a part of it. What had started as a personal endeavor and dream had taken on a much bigger meaning.

China has endured tumultuous events over the past century. A rebellion that overthrew the Qing dynasty ended imperial rule and established a constitutional republic in 1912. Even then, warlords controlled vast regions, including Beijing. It took 16 more years of fighting for nationalists to unify the country. War with Japan began in 1936, which was followed from 1945 by two years of civil war between nationalist and communist forces.

I was born in the 1970s, during the chaos of the Cultural Revolution, a time in which thousands of Chinese died of starvation. Since I come from that era, people see my ability to fly my own airplane around the world at age 40 as an accomplishment not just for me, but for the Chinese people. My dream is a small reflection of "Chinese Dreams," a term initiated by Communist Party leader Xi Jinping but popularized by American journalist Thomas Friedman in his article: China Needs Its Own Dream.

Xi's Chinese Dream is described as achieving the "Two 100s": the material goal of China becoming a "moderately well-off society" by about 2020, the 100th anniversary of the Chinese Communist Party, and the goal of China becoming a fully developed nation by about 2049, the 100th anniversary of the founding of the People's Republic.

Xi called upon young people to "dare to dream, work assiduously to fulfill the dreams and contribute to the revitalization of the nation." According to Robert Lawrence Kuhn, the Chinese Dream has four parts: Strong China (economically, politically, diplomatically, scientifically, militarily); Civilized China (equity and fairness, rich culture, high morals); Harmonious China (amity among social classes); Beautiful China (healthy environment, low pollution). Khun states that "a moderately well-off society" is where all citizens, rural and urban, enjoy high standards of living. This includes doubling the 2010 per capita GDP (approaching $10,000) by about 2020 and completing urbanization (roughly one billion people, 70 percent of China's population) by about 2030. "Modernization" means China regaining its position as a world leader in science and technology as well as in economics and business; the resurgence of Chinese civilization, culture and military might; and China participating actively in all areas of human endeavor.

The concept of Chinese Dream is very similar to the idea of the "American Dream." It stresses the importance of entrepreneurial spirit. It also glorifies a generation of self-made men and women in post-reform China such as rural immigrants who moved to urban centers and achieved magnificent improvement in terms of their living standards and social lives.

America embraces a foreigner like me coming to the U.S. and pursuing my "American Dream" through entrepreneurship. This is what made America the No. 1 country in the world. The adoption of "Chinese Dream" by young Chinese people will ensure China to continue its road to prosperity.

Knowing I had kicked off the trip with a fund-raiser for St. Jude Children's Research Hospital, my friend Wu told me there were many children in Southeast Asia who needed help. We should do something for them, he said. I agreed. Within one day, Mr. Wu found a poor elementary school outside Vientiane, Laos, and an orphanage in Ho Chi Minh City, Vietnam. Both needed a lot of financial help. I flew to both places, and Mr. Wu joined us.

After we landed in Laos, we bought school bags for every pupil in the elementary school we were to visit. The next morning, a relentless monsoon rain was pelting the earth. The school was about a two-hour drive into countryside. The road was unpaved, and only the driver's skill kept us from sliding off it. When we finally arrived, we saw a one-story building barely capable of providing shelter for the children to study. About 40 kids, aged five to nine, sat in a classroom waiting for us. Their clothes were worn but clean.

They didn't understand why we were there, but as we handed a school bag to each child and gave each a hug, their faces lit up. We had blue bags for boys and pink ones for girls. This was probably the only school bag they ever had, and we could sense their happiness.

We gave the principal a large donation to help support the school. She was a middle-aged woman with a big heart and a positive attitude. She dedicated her life to educating kids in the impoverished countryside. She gave hope to children who most needed it and opened doors to better futures, which in turn meant a better future for their country. Her sacrifice earned our deepest respect.

From Laos, we flew to Ho Chi Minh City. After landing in the evening, we bought food and early the next morning went to the orphanage Mr. Wu had found. It cared for 30 to 40 children, aged from two or three to as old as 15 or 16 with more girls than boys. The manager was also a middle-aged woman with a lot of enthusiasm. She explained where the children came from and how the orphanage managed to stay running. With little government support, it relied mostly on donations. We gave her a large sum of money along with our admiration of her dedication to these children.

She showed us around the narrow, four-floor building. We met all the orphans and gave them the food we brought. Even though we couldn't communicate verbally, we played with the kids for a good part of the day. On the third floor, we saw a boy alone studying. He wasn't giving in to the terrible challenges of his life. He had dreams for himself.

We all had our own dreams when we were young. Some wanted to become successful entrepreneurs, some wanted to make the world a better place, and some wanted to revolutionize industries. Few of us pursued our dreams when we grew older, mostly because of the challenges and difficulties. When we gave up our dreams, our lives would never reach the height we expected.

The greatest people in history all had dreams and never gave up no matter how difficult the dreams were. Dr. Martin Luther King's "I Have a Dream" speech, has laid the foundation of a strong America. Nobel Peace Prize winner, Muhammad Yunus dreamed of helping the poor and invented the "Microfinancing Model" benefiting millions of poor people. Apple's co-founder, Steve Jobs, said "We live to change the world."

St. Jude Childrens' Research Hospital was found by Danny Thomas with a dream that "No Child should die in the dawn of life." Danny Thomas was a struggling young comic when he met Rose Marie Mantell, who had a singing career with her own radio show in Detroit, Michigan. When Rose Marie was about to give birth to their first child, Marlo, Danny Thomas was torn between his dedication to his work and his responsibility to his family.

Desperate, Danny put his last $7 in the offering bin and knelt before the statute of St. Jude, the patron saint of the hopeless and prayed for a sign to guide his way in life. He promised to erect a shrine to St. Jude if he became successful. Just shortly after one week, Danny Thomas signed a contract for $500 per week at 5100 Club in Chicago. Danny went on to become one of the best-loved entertainers of his time, starring in shows in New York and Chicago, Hollywood movies and in the television series "Make Room for Daddy," which became one of the most successful and honored family comedy shows in television history.

Throughout his successes, Danny never forgot his promise to St. Jude. In 1957, Thomas founded the American Lebanese Syrian

Associated Charities (ALSAC), the fundraising organization of St. Jude. Danny gave of himself wholeheartedly in the effort to realize his dream, contributing his talents, time and money. ALSAC became one of the most successful fundraising organizations in American history.

The mission statement of St. Jude Children's Research Hospital is "to advance cures, and means of prevention, for pediatric catastrophic diseases through research and treatment." Discoveries at St. Jude have completely changed how doctors treat children with cancer and other catastrophic illnesses. Since St. Jude was established, the survival rate for acute lymphoblastic leukemia, the most common type of childhood cancer, has increased from 4 percent in 1962 to 94 percent today. During this time, the overall survival rate for childhood cancers has risen from 20 percent to 80 percent.

St. Jude has treated more than 20,000 children from across the U.S. and more than 70 foreign countries. Its International Outreach program is organized to improve survival rates of children worldwide through the transfer of knowledge, technology and skills. It depends heavily on donations and has remained true to Thomas's dream that no child will be turned away based on a family's inability to pay.

In 1996, Peter C. Doherty, PhD, won the Nobel prize for medicine based on immunology research he performed at St. Jude. That is only one of hundreds of scientific and humanitarian awards associated with the hospital's staff and supporters. Danny Thomas himself was awarded the Congressional Gold Medal in 1985 and his daughter Marlo was presented with the Jefferson award in 2011 for lifetime achievement.

St. Jude is organized to transfer researchers discoveries from the lab to the bedside as quickly as possible. It was listed as one of the 10 best places to work for seven straight years in *Scientist*. And one of the 100 best companies to work for by Fortune magazine in 2011, 2012 and 2013. It not only gives its personnel freedom to dream, it is structured to turn those dreams into real world solutions efficiently.

A dream isn't a passing fancy; it's a life's quest.

Even though I undertook my flight around the world to fulfill a personal goal, a very important aspect of that adventure and of this book was not only to raise funds, but also to increase awareness of work being done at the research hospital.

Visiting the elementary school and the orphanage was a humbling experience, as I could see myself in their situation. It reminded me of what I had been through, and evoked vivid memories of my own school and life. Looking at where I was then and comparing it to where I am now, I feel not only graced by fortune, but also gifted with the responsibility to contribute where I can.

—

Every leg of the flight had its own challenge. When we flew from Vientiane, Laos, to Ho Chi Minh City, Vietnam, we encountered extreme turbulence in a thunderstorm. In the U.S., we can access weather information on board that would enable us to avoid thunderstorms. Here we had no such information.

When we took off in the morning, the weather was good until we entered clouds about 30 minutes from Ho Chi Minh City.

Looking down, I saw a massive thunderstorm beneath us. There was no way around it. As we neared the airport, we had no choice but to descend.

Mr. Wu was sitting in the back, along with a cameraman from CCTV, Chang Zheng, and a news reporter from Beijing, Li Ye, to document the flight. They were "lucky" to pick this leg. I told everybody to fasten seatbelts and expect violent turbulence. As we began our descent, I switched off the autopilot, so I could fly the plane manually. The cameraman had an old-style camcorder with a big battery on the back. He tried to videotape the moment, and the plane jerked so violently the battery fell out.

I had to slow down to maneuver speed (Va) at 158 Knots, to make sure the structure of the airplane wasn't damaged. I didn't try to fight the turbulence. Pilots can get into trouble if we try to counter turbulence and maintain a level flight. It could overstress the airframe and break the wings off. I let the turbulence carry the airplane wherever it wanted to go, 200 feet up, then 200 feet down not fighting it, just going through it. My luggage in the back went from floor to ceiling, up and down. I could hear my passengers screaming. It's always worse for the passengers, as they are not in control. They probably thought the wings would be torn off. We were in the turbulence for a little more than five minutes, but it seemed like hours. When we finally made it through the storm and landed safely at Ho Chi Minh City Airport, I was glad that no one had puked in the airplane.

From Vietnam, we flew to Hong Kong on July 4. Landing at Hong Kong International Airport needed a slot time reservation. I made a reservation at 2 p.m. and had to arrive within plus or minus

10 minutes. We took off earlier in order to give us plenty of time to adjust our speed for the wind. We could always slow down if the wind was in our favor and the flight took less time. But we couldn't speed up if the wind was against us and we were late. At exactly 2 p.m., we were at the glide scope of the runway and cleared to land at the beautiful airport in the harbor. The newly completed airport deserved the $15 million liability insurance I bought.

The Hong Kong Aviation Club (HKAC) gave me a welcome. John Lee, the president, took me on a helicopter ride over Hong Kong. A helicopter ride is always the best treat for a pilot. I had been to Hong Kong many, many times but had never seen it from above. I'd always thought it was very crowded and lacked land and space. From the air, however, Hong Kong is a beautiful city with lots of mountains and beaches. It is not crowded at all. Only 17 percent of the city's land has been developed. After the ride, we had dinner at the club's restaurant and the HKAC gave me an Honorary Lifetime Membership.

AGRA TO HONG KONG

Reception in Bangkok

From top to bottom: visiting an orphanage in Vietnam; at the Taj Mahal (left); visiting an elementary school in Laos; St. Jude Gala

FLIGHT LOG: HONG KONG TO CHANGSHA

JULY 7, 2011—JULY 10, 2011

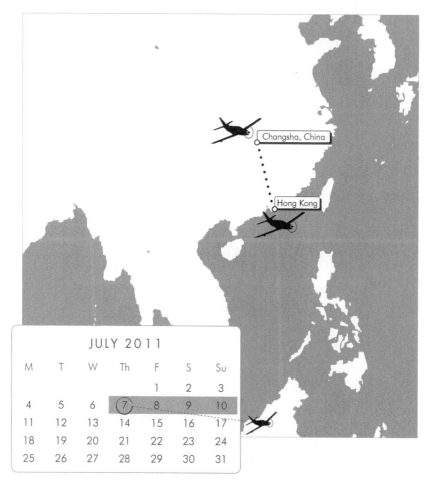

CHAPTER SIX

CHILDHOOD
(HONG KONG TO CHANGSHA)

Life is like a box of chocolates. You never know what you're gonna get."

- Forrest Gump

hen I arrived in Hong Kong on July 4, I still didn't have a permit to fly into mainland China's airspace, and our next flight was scheduled for July 7.

My friend, Earl Blankenship, a successful real estate entrepreneur in his early 50s, came to Hong Kong to join me on this leg. When I first told him about my plans to fly around the world, he thought I was nuts. Once he realized what I was trying to do, he said it was the coolest thing in the world. He wanted to take part in the most important leg of the trip – flying into mainland China's airspace.

"Wei, is everything set for the flight through China?" he asked when he welcomed me at Hong Kong International Airport. I told him that we should depart in three days, but that I didn't have clearance yet.

I started working on getting a flight permit six months before my departure from Memphis. China's airspace is divided into seven regions, each controlled by a military authority. Flying across China from Hong Kong to Russia requires coordination among five authorities.

I had contacted many of my aviation friends in China. They said they would try to help, but none of them could give me a definite answer as to whether or when I could enter. In March 2011, I met Hawk Yang, the owner of a general aviation company called China GA Links. We were born in the same year and raised in the same city. He was three months older than I. After college, I went to the U.S., and he stayed in Changsha. Our divergent paths notwithstanding, we shared a passion for flying. While I enjoyed the freedom to fly in the U.S., he fought for this freedom every day for all Chinese who loved to fly, including himself.

When we first met in Changsha, we clicked instantly and felt almost like long-lost friends. When no one else could promise to get a permit for mainland China, he was the one with the most determination. He said, "Wei, what you are doing is amazing and will become a milestone for China's aviation. We will help you fly into Chinese airspace. What a shame if the first Chinese citizen flying his own plane around the world couldn't fly into his homeland."

Not only did he agree to help me get the permit, he offered to cover all expenses in China. The flying permit and landing fees could easily exceed $12,000, at $3,000 or more per stop. To offer this to a new friend was more than just generosity; it was faith, belief, trust, and passion. While he promised to get a flight permit into the mainland, he couldn't promise to get me a permit to land at Beijing Capital International Airport.

Tragically, I lost my aviation soul mate three months after we met. On June 18, 2011, my friend Jason called to say, "Hawk Yang is missing from a river cruise. He hasn't been found." I couldn't immediately register this stark news. I had talked to Hawk Yang only two days earlier. I asked, "Who is missing?" Jason said again that it was Hawk Yang. I couldn't speak. After a few seconds, I said, "He is just missing, right? Maybe a rescue team will find him." I still didn't want to believe he might never be found.

Jason told me that the rescue team had been searching for 24 hours. As long as they hadn't found his body, he might have survived, I thought. I told Jason we had to pray for him. I kept my fingers crossed. Three days later, the rescue team found his body. He drowned after his legs caught in waterweeds. He left behind a beautiful wife, a three-year-old child, and many friends who miss him terribly.

After his death, his partner, Liangjun Liu, along with help from China's Aircraft Owners and Pilots Association (AOPA), continued working on getting a permit for me. Every week, I would check with Liu on the status. His answer was always positive, but he couldn't confirm the permit would be granted. The CAAC requested more and more documents about the airplane, as no Socata TBM had ever flown into China before. This airplane was not in their system.

As time passed in Hong Kong, I became more and more concerned. I hadn't prepared an alternative flight path as I was determined to fly into China's airspace. I had no time to work out a different route, because I would have had to get visas for all the countries I would enter. My Russian visa would expire soon.

Then on July 5 at 2 p.m., I got a call in the hotel lobby from Mr. Liu. "Wei," he said, "we got the permit." Excitement rang in his voice. I asked him to send the details. When I opened his email with the permit, I saw ZBAA, the code for Beijing Capital International Airport. Not only was I going to fly into China's restricted airspace, I was also cleared to land at Beijing Capital International Airport. I jumped off my seat, screamed, laughed and almost cried.

I immediately shared the news with my aviation friends in the U.S. and Europe. Before leaving Hong Kong, AOPA in the U.S. interviewed me for an article in the association's Pilot's Magazine. *(See editor's note for Web link.) The highlight of the interview was when they asked me whether I could fly into China's airspace, which was essentially barred to private airplanes. When I answered "yes," they were delighted. China was opening its airspace to general aviation. When the airplane's manufacturer, Daher-Socata, heard this news it issued an immediate news release: "A TBM 700 becomes the first general aviation aircraft to fly across China to Beijing."

The morning of July 7, I, along with Earl Blankenship and my brother, Andy Chen, took off for the mainland.

The moment Hong Kong's ATC handed me over to China's ATC, I became excited. I reported my altitude and heading, then immediately asked the controller for his name. I told him that since the day I started flying, I had been waiting for this moment. "Thank you for being part of a cherished event in my life," I told him. He was curious to know who I was. I explained that I was flying around the world and this was my first time to enter Chinese airspace. He'd never seen my type of airplane in the system and asked what kind of aircraft it was and how long it had been since I'd begun my trip.

It was a remarkable moment – I felt like laughing and crying at the same time. I had to calm myself and focus on flying. As we neared Changsha and heard the Changsha tower on the radio, I requested a conversation with the controller. After learning the purpose of the flight, he gave me an exclusive frequency. I explained my excitement was because I was born and reared in Changsha. He could scarcely believe I was flying around the world in my own airplane. We spoke in our local dialect, the coolest dialogue on the air.

Even after getting my pilot's license, I had hardly dared to dream that one day I would land my own airplane at Changsha airport.

—

I was born in 1971 in the midst of China's Cultural Revolution, which spanned 10 years from 1966 to 1976. In my opinion and the opinion of many others, that was the nation's darkest time since the communist victory in 1949. It was presaged by the Great Leap Forward from 1958 to 1961, which was intended to transform China from an agrarian to an industrial society by abolishing private farming. Instead of advancing development, an estimated 18 to 45 million people starved to death. At that time moderate leaders, including Deng Xiaoping became more powerful while

Mao Zedong was becoming marginalized. In response, a cadre of party leaders loyal to Mao launched China's Cultural Revolution.

Traditional society was turned on its head with students taking over schools and denigrating their teachers. Even many party members were targeted by their former comrades. Factional struggles spread. Millions of people were persecuted in violence that engulfed the country. They suffered abuses, public humiliation, arbitrary imprisonment, torture, sustained harassment, and seizure of property.

The country fell into even greater poverty amid the violence. Teachers and intellectuals were imprisoned, and schools were closed down. My mom and dad didn't finish high school because their school closed. They had no opportunity for education. My mom started her first part-time job in the summer at the age of 11. She worked as a factory laborer and made $3 per month. My dad started working at 17 at an automotive parts factory.

My parents met through a mutual friend's introduction, while they were working at different factories. They fell in love instantly and had me unexpectedly when my mom was only 16 years old. While abortion in China was a common practice, my mom and dad decided to keep me, even when they barely had anything to eat themselves. They married before I was born, and the wedding gift was just a set of old furniture from my dad's older brother.

When I was born, my mom was 17 and my dad was 21. They were still kids themselves and hardly had time to take care of me while working at the factory and trying to make ends meet. My parents had no choice but to send me to live with family members in the countryside. Accompanied by my great-grandpa, I went to a rural area, where people farmed to feed themselves and food was not as scarce. I became my great-grandpa's favorite boy, and he brought me everywhere he went. I stayed in the country until I was six and saw my mom and dad only once every other year.

Life in the country was fun for a kid. I rode cows, fed chickens and pigs, picked dry wood from the forest, planted wheat and played in the river. I tried to catch fish but rarely had luck. Rice with soy sauce was my favorite dish. Meat was available only once a year during the Chinese Spring Festival, when a pig was killed to feed the whole village. There were many children and we had no school, no rules, and no worries. For us the whole area was a playground of mountains, river, farmland, and our backyards. The Cultural Revolution imposed scarcely endurable hardship on Chinese people, but as for children in our village, we knew nothing about it and were not old enough to care.

When Chairman Mao died on September 9, 1976, the Cultural Revolution ended. In 1977, I moved back to the city and was reunited with my mom and dad. City life was strange to me at the beginning. There was little space to play, and the kids were not as friendly. I was viewed as a hick, with unsophisticated style and a strong country accent.

I started elementary school at the age of 7. Although my parents did not have an opportunity for education, they knew its importance. The rural area where I'd been living didn't have an education system, but in the city I was able to enroll in elementary school.

When I started, my mom was 24 years old and had been working full time for almost 10 years. No matter how hard her life was, she never complained or whined about anything. She always had the most positive attitude toward life. She felt proud of her ability to work at a very young age to help support her family. Although she didn't have a chance to finish high school, she never stopped learning and went to night and weekend classes. She always had a smile and lightened everyone's mood when she entered a room.

My mom emphasized two things to me: positive attitude and sense of pride. She always made us look good in front of others. Even though our clothes were old and worn, they were always clean and well kept. She made sure our house was tidy when we had guests. Even though food was scarce, we always had plenty available for guests, even if it meant Mom had to spend our last penny. She never grumbled about hardships. She felt blessed that we had a better life than many others and was confident that things would get better – and they did.

In the 1980s, our lives improved. I watched TV for the first time. My family, along with 30 to 40 other people, would gather to watch a nine-inch black and white TV in our neighbor's house. I first learned of a country called "America" through the TV series *Garrison's Gorillas*. Garrison, the show's hero, became a "role model" for me and all my friends. I was dying to get a pair of sunglasses like his, even though I couldn't afford them. I got a small knife and practiced throwing it at a tree, hoping it would stick, straight and deep. I started to smoke like Garrison, and I believed fighting for your friends was heroic.

The TV series led to "gangster" fighting among youths. I had many friends and because I was taller than most kids my age, my friends loved to ask me to fight for them. As a kid, there was nothing better than feeling that you could help a friend, and that you were the "Big Brother" in the group. That feeling ended one day, when we lost a fight. I ended up with 20 stitches in my head and almost got myself killed. When I went home, my mom cried, but she didn't reprimand me for what I'd done. She just took really good care of me.

When I finished high school, I didn't want to go to college. I wanted to start working like my parents. I was hardly a top student and had only average scores. I didn't like Chinese teaching style, which is boring and not interactive. My mom had a long talk with me and told me how important education was. She regretted that she didn't have the chance for higher education. She insisted that I go to college and she promised it would change my life. I did, and it did.

College was much more fun than high school. I started to enjoy learning, to some degree. The classes were more interactive and the activities were more fun. I stayed in a dorm with eight guys in a 300-square-foot room. There was no air conditioner in summer and no heater in winter. There was no private bathroom. All 200 students on the floor shared one big shower room. The toilets smelled awful. Still I was very happy with dorm life and made many great friends.

American movies became very popular in China in the early '90s. The movie, *Forrest Gump*, inspired me the most. I watched it three times. I was astounded at how Forrest, with an IQ of 75, could accomplish so many great things in his life. It taught me that, if I wanted to be successful in anything, the number one thing was to be persistent just like Forrest was with running, ping pong, and shrimping. It taught me that everyone had challenges that they had to overcome in life, but how you responded to them made the difference. It taught me that life was just like the flying feather at the beginning and conclusion of the movie that we could fly far away and could land anywhere.

In the same year that *Forrest Gump* came out, China broadcasted the popular TV series *A Native of Beijing in New York*. It was the story of a poor Beijing musician and his wife who after longing for America for many years finally went to New York to pursue the American Dream. After struggling in the beginning, the musician eventually became a successful businessman, but at the cost of giving up his music and divorcing his wife.

It was at this time that I first had the desire to go to America. My mom was very supportive of this idea. Her boss's son was in New York attending a university, and she had heard about all the great things in the U.S. Not really knowing what the country was like or what I would do once I got there, I started to work toward my goal. To go to the U.S. for higher education, I needed to study English. I had to pass the TOEFL, the Test of English as a Foreign Language, before any school could admit me. I spent 16 hours a day for the next three months preparing for this test and got a very good score on it, even though I still could hardly speak any English. Then I asked for help from my cousin, Bing Ye, who was a PhD student in the U.S., to assist me in applying to universities. My application to North Carolina State University was accepted. The school sent me a Certificate of Eligibility for Nonimmigrant Student Status (Form I-20), which is necessary to receive a U.S. student visa.

In the early '90s, getting a U.S. visa was like winning a lottery. After I received Form I-20 from the university, I prepared all my documents and went to the U.S. Embassy in Guangzhou to interview for a student visa.

I arrived in Guangzhou a day before my scheduled interview date. The next morning, I awoke early and went to the U.S. Embassy. I thought I would be the early bird, but hundreds of people were already waiting in line. Everyone was chatting about their experiences on applying for the visas. When someone came out of the embassy, he or she would be surrounded by people anxiously asking how the interview officer felt that day. I waited for a few hours before passing through security and entering the waiting room. It was very quiet even though about 100 people stood in different lines. Everyone appeared nervous. After few more hours, my number was called. The officer looked at my application and asked a few questions. The interview was over in less than two minutes, and my application was rejected.

When I went back to my hometown, I didn't know what to do. I thought about giving up the dream of going to the U.S. After all, I had a good job at a Hunan Provincial Import & Export agency and a very caring boss with a bright future. Our business of exporting canned fruits was growing very rapidly. I loved my job, and my life was comfortable.

However, I couldn't do it. I couldn't disappoint my mom. I needed to try again. After one more month of preparation, I decided to go to the Beijing Embassy. I wasn't sure whether a different embassy would change my fate, but I would give it my best. I had heard of someone who tried six or seven times before getting a visa. This time, I came better prepared to answer questions, so I was more confident than before, and more relaxed. This time, I got an F-1 student visa to the United States of America.

I called my mom as soon as I walked out of the embassy. She couldn't have been happier and screamed with joy. She believed in Buddhism and had prayed for me that morning. She thanked Buddha for making it happen. I was happy that I'd made her proud.

I really didn't know anything about the U.S. and didn't know what my future would look like. In my 24 years, I had never been abroad. Although I passed the TOEFL, I could hardly speak English. I had to leave my friends behind and start a new life in a strange country. I didn't know what this "American Dream" meant, but I was eager to accept the challenge and adventure.

America here I come!

—

When we landed in Changsha, my high school teachers brought more than 100 students from senior classes to the airport to welcome me and asked me to share my story. My teachers could hardly recognize me after 20 years, but I immediately spotted my class teacher, Xiao Jiangping, in the crowd of hundreds. His smile, which was engraved in my brain, had not changed in 20 years. I had the opportunity to meet with all of my high school teachers for the first time since I graduated in 1990.

The next day, we toured my high school's new campus. What a difference two decades had made. The classrooms, playground, basketball court, the library, all were state-of-the-art. The students wore uniforms. I was overwhelmed.

I stayed in Changsha for two days. During the trip, I was able to see my grandpa who had been diagnosed with late-stage cancer and had only months to live. It was the last time I would see him. Our youngest daughter had never been to China. Isabel brought all three of our daughters to Changsha, so my grandfather could see them before he passed away three months later.

My father's 61st birthday was July 9, 2011. The timing was perfect and made the trip even more meaningful. We all celebrated Dad's birthday together, making the family reunion an event that remains particularly dear in my memory.

• *NOTE: A* Pilot's Magazine *article about the Beijing landing includes a video interview with Wei Chen and Yinjie Jason Zhang made before Wei's takeoff from Memphis:*

http://www.aopa.org/News-and-video/All-News/2011/July/14/cleared-to-land-Beijing-touchdown-a-first-for-GA-in-China.aspx

• *Extensive Web coverage can be found under a search: Wei's trip around the world*

CHANGSHA

Wei in Changsha

Reception in Changsha

With family in Changsha

FLIGHT LOG: CHANGSHA TO BEIJING

JULY 10, 2011—JULY 15, 2011

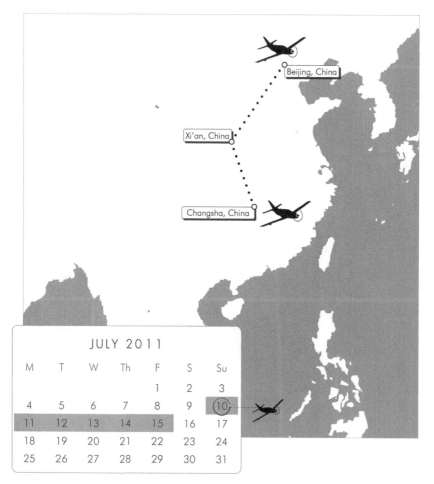

Beijing, China

Xi'an, China

Changsha, China

JULY 2011

M	T	W	Th	F	S	Su
				1	2	3
4	5	6	7	8	9	10
11	12	13	14	15	16	17
18	19	20	21	22	23	24
25	26	27	28	29	30	31

CHAPTER SEVEN

"CLEARED TO LAND AT BEIJING"
(CHANGSHA TO BEIJING)

Never, never, never give up.

- Winston Churchill

lthough I had a permit to land at Beijing Capital International Airport, I almost missed achieving one of my primary goals on my descent to the runway.

When I was cleared to land in Beijing on July 5, 2011, I shared the news with the airplane's manufacturer, Daher-Socata in France. They published a news release for "this historic flight and new chapter in general aviation history."

Beijing Capital International Airport is the second busiest airport in the world and the busiest airport in China. In 2011, it accommodated more than 78 million passengers and more than

530,000 takeoffs and landings for a daily average of 1,460 flights in and out. Given a 16-hour working day, there was a landing and takeoff every 40 seconds. However, CAAC's policy states that any airport with more than 200 takeoffs and landings was considered a busy airport, and single-engine airplanes were banned.

When I initially expressed my dream of landing at Beijing Capital International Airport, everyone thought I was crazy and this dream was impossible. I would be lucky if CAAC would let me fly across China's airspace. "Don't even think about it!" People laughed at this dream.

It was not just one person we had to persuade to let us land at Beijing airport. We had to persuade everyone in the system and explain the significance of the landing as well as the risks associated with it. Everyone we talked to understood that it would be a historic landing. No one wanted to reject our proposal. However, people were wary of the professional risk of approving it. Something might go wrong, or some obscure regulation might be violated. They were not familiar with my airplane, so people involved requested all kinds of documents about it, including noise abatement.

I was befuddled. How could a single-engine airplane make more noise than a Boeing 777? It didn't matter. We patiently submitted all documents as per each CAAC request.

Over the course of my trip, I felt like a climber of Mount Everest. The closer I got to China, the closer I came to the summit. Like an expedition to scale the world's tallest mountain, all conditions — weather, snow, and equipment — had to be right, as does the timing. You have to wait for the right moment to make that climb, if you want to reach the top and come back safely. Even though

I had the piloting ability to land at Beijing Capital International Airport, the more critical matters were getting CAAC personnel to understand my single-engine airplane's capability, to think outside the box and to take a professional risk.

Anyone in the chain of approval could easily have said "No," and that would have been the end of it. They didn't have to imperil their careers on the hope I had the ability to land without messing up anything. If I made one mistake during the landing that delayed traffic at Beijing Capital International Airport, it would have been exceedingly bad international news. With a plane landing every 40 seconds, my mistake could create a major air traffic delay for the whole country. That's a tremendous risk for the official who finally signs off on that permit. He had to trust my ability and believe it was the right thing to do for China's general aviation in order to risk his career.

I knew this special landing permit was a result of a few months of tough lobbying efforts and smart navigation through a sea of regulations by Mr. Liu and Zhi Jie at AOPA China.

When I looked closely at the flight permit, I saw it called for me to depart Xi'an at 9 p.m. and arrive at Beijing at midnight. By having me fly at night, CAAC personnel sought to mitigate their risk. If something happened, it wouldn't create chaos for commercial travel during the day. However, I didn't want to fly at night across unfamiliar terrain and land at the second largest airport in the dark.

After landing at Changsha, I asked Mr. Liu to request an amendment to the flight time. He thought I was crazy. How could I put this most significant landing at risk? I told him that safety was the utmost concern for the authority in granting the landing permit. If they wanted to do all they could do to minimize risk, they should allow me to land in daylight, not at midnight. He said he would try again.

No effort is made in vain. The CAAC agreed to change my flight time and requested that I take off at 5 a.m. from Xi'an and land at Beijing Capital International Airport no later than 8 a.m., before traffic got heavy. Taking off in the dark didn't cause me nearly as much concern as landing at one of the busiest airports in the world at midnight. I agreed and accepted the new flight time with great relief.

On July 11, I went to bed at eight o'clock, missing a banquet that had been planned for me. I declined the hospitality and asked for forgiveness. I couldn't take any risk that might endanger the flight.

I set the wake-up call for 4 a.m., to give us plenty of time to get to the airport and be ready to depart at 5 a.m. At three o'clock, the phone rang. The handler told me that Beijing was concerned about this flight and requested that we depart one hour earlier than planned. That meant we needed to arrive at the airport at 4 a.m. I said fine. I had seven hours' sleep and felt good and was glad that I was prepared for the unexpected.

When we got to the airport, Alan Hepburn, my co-pilot, said he didn't think it was safe to fly. He was one of four co-pilots I hired to help navigate. While he was a tremendous asset in crossing the Atlantic Ocean, he put a huge amount of pressure on me for this most significant leg.

He said he hadn't enough sleep, as he'd stayed up until midnight. Because we moved the departure time one hour earlier, he also believed taking off in total darkness was unsafe. I told him I'd had enough sleep and felt good, so I could fly by myself if need be. Jason also volunteered to co-pilot this historic leg. However, I didn't think it was the best idea to change the co-pilot in the last minute and create uncertainty in everyone's mind.

Then I changed the subject and suggested we check the weather to see if it was okay. I knew that most pilots' biggest concern is bad weather. If the weather were okay, that would give him confidence. I already knew the weather was good, since I had checked it the night before. Changing the subject removed the tension. After checking the weather, Alan felt much better and agreed that it was safe to fly. I was relieved to hear that and moved on. I needed to put all my personal feelings aside and focus on this flight.

We arrived at the tarmac at 4:30 a.m., half an hour late due to the distraction. We agreed to wait 15 minutes more and depart at 4:45 a.m., ensuring that we had some visibility when we took off. At 4:45 a.m. sharp, we cranked up the engine and requested departure from the tower. The tower operator said, "I have been waiting for you for all night. Congratulations on your trip." I realized that the whole airport had been kept open over night just for my flight. That was quite an unexpected honor.

The departure was smooth, even in the dark. When we climbed above the clouds, we could see that it was a beautiful day to fly. About 30 minutes into the flight, sunlight began tinting the clouds in magnificent color, creating the most exquisite sunrise I had ever seen. Admittedly, I may have been biased by my excitement, but it was undeniably beautiful. After taking in the view, I focused on flying. I knew we were being watched closely. Any mistake could result in being re-routed to the alternative airport in Tianjin, which is a half hour from Beijing Capital International Airport.

At 7:20 a.m., I was 100 nautical miles and 20 minutes away from the Beijing airport and ATC requested that I start descending. I listened to ATIS, Automatic Terminal Information Service, at Beijing Capital International Airport. It gave me weather information on the airport and expected runway. The weather looked fine, with a 2,000 foot ceiling and good visibility. Perfect for an easy visual landing, I told myself.

When the ATC transited me to Beijing tower, the controller began by welcoming me to Beijing. Again, I was reminded that my flight was closely watched. The controller asked me to join ILS approach as soon as practical, even though I was 30 nautical miles away. Being able to join ILS earlier gave me more time to establish my airplane on the approach in the speed and glide ratio that I was most comfortable with. I had more than 10 minutes to adjust my airplane to a perfect gliding condition. It was a luxury that I expected to make for an easy landing.

As I descended and got closer to the runway, I flew into clouds or heavy fog. I couldn't tell the difference. Beijing is almost always foggy in the morning. I'd expected a cloud ceiling at 2,000 feet above ground, so that I'd be able to see the runway when I was five nautical miles and three minutes away. However, at just 1,000 feet and 90 seconds from the airport, I was still in clouds, or fog. Nothing was visible but haze. I continued to descend at the designated glide ratio with my flaps and landing gear extended. I focused on my instruments and made sure my airplane was on the glide slope. If I were above or below the glide slope, then I would never make the runway.

In the ILS approach, there is an absolute minimum altitude, called "Decision Altitude." The normal Decision Altitude for an ILS approach is about 200 feet above ground. At this altitude, we would be only 15 seconds away from touchdown. If we were still in the clouds and couldn't see the runway, we would have to start a "Missed Approach" and go around. Otherwise, the landing was illegal and would be too dangerous. I'm a conservative pilot. Normally I set my personal Decision Altitude at 600 feet above ground for an ILS approach, which would give me 45 seconds to touchdown. Safety is the utmost concern.

On that day, however, I had to extend my acceptable level of risk. I knew that, if for whatever reason I declared a Missed Approach and went around, ATC might re-route me to Tianjin Airport. If I executed a Missed Approach, I would miss the 8 a.m. deadline and ATC might not let me come back.

My heart pounded as I searched for visual sighting of the runway, while staying focused on the instruments. We started to count the airplane's altitude above ground: 800 feet, 600 feet, 400 feet. My hands moved to the throttle to get ready for a Missed Approach, regardless of my determination. I would have missed a historic landing at Beijing Capital International Airport. That inescapably would have disappointed the many people who had worked hard to make it happen. It would imbue a negative image on general aviation that while a big airplane could land in this kind of weather with Category II and Category III capability, a small airplane could not.

When we reached 300 feet, three seconds from Decision Altitude, I saw the high-intensity runway lights. I shouted, "I got it, I got it!" These lights are used to outline runways during darkness or limited visibility. I knew I had made the runway when I saw these lights. My hand relaxed on the throttle and my heart regained its normal rhythm. I continued gliding and touched down on the runway smoothly. To me it was the best landing ever.

Once I taxied off the runway, everyone on the plane was shouting, "We made it! We made it!" We all knew it was a historic moment. As we taxied among big commercial airplanes, the Boeings and the Airbuses, the sense of pride and excitement of making history were evident among everyone in the airplane. It was special to share this extraordinary moment with John Chen, my brother from another mother; Earl Blankenship, my closest American friend; and Jason Zhang, a passionate Chinese aviator.

After we disembarked, we had to go through security. When processing the paperwork, the security guard asked which airline I was flying for. My being the first single-engine private airplane allowed to land there, I worried that filling out forms could cause trouble. The security guard didn't know how to fill in all the blanks designed for airline operators.

Once we made it through security, I was greeted by the president of AOPA China who gave me a big hug and congratulated me on my historic landing. He played a significant role in helping obtain the flight permit as did his associate, Zhi Jie, who had lobbied the CAAC hard for months. We posed for a picture in front of a long red banner that read, "A milestone in China's general aviation history, and the start of new era."

Many aviation enthusiasts came to the airport to witness the landing. A young guy, probably about 20 years old, said, "I flew from Xiamen to Beijing just to meet you. You are my hero!" He introduced himself, Cheng Chi, a student pilot at Civil Aviation Flight University of China. Because of his parents' influence, he loved aviation from early age and even practiced flying around the world with a flight simulator. Then, all he asked for was a picture with me. I hugged him and gave the best smile I could for the photo.

Beijing is the capital of China. With a population of more than 20 million, it is the nation's second largest city after Shanghai. I stayed in Beijing for three days, giving several interviews a day to reporters from local newspapers and national TV.

The Chinese central government agency, Qiao Liang, hosted a lavish banquet to celebrate the trip and landing at Beijing Capital International Airport. The same agency organized an official news conference in Beijing on March 9, 2011, two months before my departure, and sent the performance group to various cities along my route.

Minister Qiao Wei joined the banquet and congratulated me. In a speech, he said the Chinese people were proud of what I had accomplished and that it inspired patriotism among all the people we had touched. The message of "Embrace China, Happy Flying" was well received around the world. He talked about China's recent history and how it has grown to become the second largest economy in the world. However, China remains a developing country and there are many opportunities and challenges ahead of us. The only way China can continue its prosperity is to unite Chinese around the world and work toward the same goal.

"Each Chinese organization around the world is like a pearl," he said, "and your flight is thread. It connects the pearls together and makes a necklace."

Indeed, it was my honor and privilege to carry this message.

What China has accomplished in the last thirty years since it reformed its economy is truly remarkable. When Deng Xiaoping rose to power in 1978, he began moving the country away from central planning and introduced aspects of capitalism. China's investment- and export-led economy has grown about 35-fold. It is the world's fastest growing major economy, with growth rates averaging 10 percent over the past 30 years.

Now, it is the world's second largest economy, with an estimated gross domestic product of more than $8.35 trillion, according to World Bank data. China has not only provided millions of people opportunities to build wealth, more importantly, it has significantly improved the living standards of the country's 1.3 billion people, 20 percent of the world's population.

—

On July 10, prior to the flight from Xi'an to Beijing, I flew from Changsha to Xi'an with my dad, Jason Zhang, and Earl Blankenship. It would normally be a two-hour flight, but we had to detour to the northeast to avoid a military base. The flight took four hours, and we crossed both the Yangtze and the Yellow Rivers. I dreamt about flying over these rivers every time I flew over the Mississippi River near Memphis.

Xi'an is the hub of China's general aviation. It is known as the city of aerospace science and technology. The Xi'an National Civil Aerospace Industrial Base was established there on December 26, 2007. When the base's administrative committee learned about my plan to become the first Chinese citizen to fly a single-engine airplane around the world, they asked me to stop in Xi'an, if possible. I quickly agreed. There was no better way for me to promote China's general aviation than to land at its pioneer city.

The administrative committee arranged a wonderful welcome reception for us. It included a parade of 40 high school students playing drums and singing as I walked off the airplane. That was followed by an official news conference and a banquet. I met with all the kids and gave each of them a souvenir from Memphis. When I asked them whether they wanted to become future pilots, they all yelled, "Yes!" I hoped many of them could follow through and become aviators.

The news conference was organized to present an award to me and to acknowledge the historic significance of the trip and the importance of Xi'an in promoting general aviation in China. The city has significant aviation resources. It is home to more than 100 aviation companies, including the largest aircraft manufacturer in China. A quarter of the nation's aviation resources reside in Xi'an. Pucheng General Aviation Park of Xi'an hosts the nation's biggest general aviation event, the biennial China International General Aviation Convention (CIGAC), which attracts about 150,000 visitors.

BEIJING

With John Chen in Beijing

On the ground in Beijing

From top to bottom: reception in Beijing;
news conference in Xi'an; reception in Xi'an

FLIGHT LOG: BEIJING TO MEMPHIS

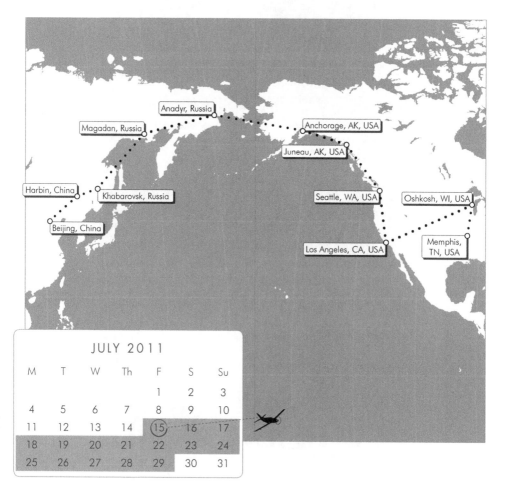

CHAPTER EIGHT

WELCOME HOME
(BEIJING TO MEMPHIS)

Consideration for others is the basis of a good life, a good society.
- Confucius

The last leg in China was from Beijing to Harbin, Isabel's hometown, and she joined me on this leg. What a grand experience to bring her back to her hometown in our own airplane and fly it myself!

We made the flight on July 15, with departure scheduled for 6 a.m. The CAAC wanted us to take off before the busy time at Beijing Capital International Airport, so Isabel and I went to the airport's VIP entrance very early. Even though we were traveling in our own airplane, we had to go through security and couldn't bring any liquids, not even water. The service was great and the process was very quick. We were through in less than 10 minutes.

However, when we got to the tarmac, we were stuck for four hours. After finishing the pre-flight checklist and receiving clearance, I was ready to depart. I called ground control and requested permission to start the engine. In most Asian countries, pilots need an OK from ground control to start the engine. Ground control responded, "Engine start is not approved. We need to wait for ground clearance." I asked what the problem was. Ground control didn't respond. Maybe the controller felt he didn't need to explain the situation to me. I waited 15 minutes then called again, but I still couldn't get engine-start approval. Even though I was frustrated, I knew that it was not the time or place to argue. After all, I felt lucky that they let me land there. A little wait was not an issue.

Half an hour later, we remained stuck; one hour later, still nothing. The ground controller sensed my frustration and told me what the problem was.

The night before, a thunderstorm had hit Beijing and a lot of flights were cancelled. In the morning, many airplanes were stranded at the airport and couldn't take off. From my parking spot, I needed to taxi along a yellow line to get on the runway. The taxiway should not have been blocked for my departure, because my flight permit was approved for the morning. Unexpectedly, two big airplanes were parked ahead of me, blocking the taxiway.

I looked along the yellow line and saw that the parking spot with the Boeing 777 was only 500 feet from us. The line ran under the airliner's left wing. However, there was at least 100 feet of clearance from its left wingtip to the next airplane's right wingtip. I told ground control that my airplane's wingspan was only 41 feet. There was plenty of room for me to taxi between two big airplanes, if I strayed a little to the right of the yellow line for less than five seconds.

There was silence. Then the ground controller told me he would send someone to check it. An airport van came with a handler in uniform who measured the distance between the two airplane's wingtips; he also measured my airplane's wingspan. He agreed that there was plenty of space for me to go through safely. However, he said he couldn't make the decision and could only report his opinion to ground control.

Another 30 minutes later, I requested engine start again. Ground control still didn't approve. I told the controller that the handler had measured the space and had agreed that it was perfectly safe to go through. That met with more silence. Finally, the ground controller told me that they knew it was probably safe to let me taxi between the airplanes, but someone in authority had to approve a deviation from the yellow line. No one was willing to take the risk. Instead, they requested a tow truck to move the Boeing 777. It would take about two hours after which they could approve engine start.

At that moment, I realized again how lucky I was to have been able to land at Beijing Capital International Airport, when I couldn't get permission for a short deviation from a yellow taxi line.

Two hours later, the Boeing 777 was towed away and engine start was approved. We were four hours behind schedule. Luckily, I was in no rush, and the flight from Beijing to Harbin was only two and a half hours. We were hungry while waiting, and the ground handlers were nice enough to send us food because we couldn't go out to the lounge again.

When I finally started the engine, I carefully stayed right in the center of the yellow taxi line. I wanted to make sure I didn't deviate one bit. Who knew what trouble I would be in if I missed the line by even a foot?

By then, it was already noon, the busiest time at Beijing Capital International Airport. I was taxiing among all the big Boeings and Airbuses. I had to look up from the window to see past the tops of these airplanes when I was close to them. They were so much bigger and taller, but at least in this land of giants, my airplane stood out. Here it was unique.

After all the excitement in China, the flight across Russia and the Bering Sea was long and boring. I was still more than 6,000 nautical miles from home and had only 12 days left to finish the trip. I was tired and found flying to be more physically draining than it had been at the beginning. I badly wanted to go home.

I planned three stops in Russia: Khabarovsk, Magadan, and Anadyr. There was not much to see in eastern Russia. The airport infrastructure was poor, with mud holes on taxiways, many with hand-painted detour lines to go around them. I was afraid that my tires would blow because of the rocks and holes. Fuel trucks were old, and I was concerned about the quality of Jet-A fuel. I made sure that the fuel truck drivers tested the quality before I filled the airplane myself.

After two days of nonstop flying over 3,000 nautical miles, I crossed the Bering Sea and reached Anchorage, Alaska. I became a time traveler when I crossed the International Date Line: I took off from Anadyr, Russia, on July 19 and arrived at Anchorage, Alaska, on July 18, rolling my watch back 20 hours.

When people ask me how long it took to fly around the world. I always say 69 days, counting from May 22 to July 29, 2011. However, counting the two July 18ths, the total was almost 70 days.

Once I was back in the U.S., even though it was Alaska, I knew my mission would be accomplished. All the hard parts were over. Flying in the U.S. was easy and fun. I tried to enjoy every stop on the rest of the journey. I planned to fly from Anchorage to Seattle, the home of Boeing; then to Los Angeles, where my cousin's family lives; then to Oshkosh, where the world's largest annual aviation event was being held. The timing couldn't have been better in that I could finish the trip with the penultimate stop at Oshkosh, a pilot's "wonderland."

In Anchorage, I flew three times around Mount McKinley, the tallest mountain in North America, with an elevation of 20,230 feet above sea level. Then I rode on a floatplane over the glaciers of Denali National Park and landed at the foot of one of the glaciers.

In Seattle, Rob Williams joined me, and we toured the Boeing factory. Through a Chinese twitter-like microblog, WeiBo, I met a Chinese couple, Shawn and Grace from Seattle, who were following my trip. Shawn, another aviation enthusiast, was also from my hometown and worked for Boeing as an engineer. When Shawn learned that my next stop was Oshkosh, he was excited and asked whether he and his wife could join me for the trip. Happily, in the U.S. adding two passengers didn't require government approval.

On July 24, Rob and I flew to Oshkosh with our new friends. Landing there was not short on challenges. The airport's control tower was the busiest in the world during the gathering, managing more than 10,000 landings within seven days. To handle this massive traffic, the handlers put four different colored dots – purple, yellow, pink, and blue – on a 6,300 foot runway, each dot was 1,500 feet apart. This allowed more than one airplane to land on the same runway at the same time.

Due to the number of planes trying to land, we were not allowed to talk to the controller. Basically, we flew a standard route for approaching a specific runway, following an airplane ahead of us at a half-mile distance. Then, when we were at the downwind, the controller would look into the sky and identify our airplane by calling the color and type. When we heard our plane identified, we acknowledged by rocking the wing.

As soon as we answered the communication by rocking, the controller gave us specific instructions to make our final turn and land at a specific spot. We landed right after the airplane in front of us, knowing there was another airplane just 1,500 feet behind us. As quickly as possible, we taxied off the runway to give the airplane behind room. A line of volunteers guided us to a specific parking spot. Upon opening the door, we were greeted with "Welcome to Oshkosh!"

My schedule was very busy and revolved around promoting Chinese general aviation to the huge gathering of aviation enthusiasts. The Experimental Aircraft Association (EAA) interviewed me about the trip for its daily newspaper. Daher-Socata had a 100th anniversary celebration during the week, and representatives from the company honored me at their news conference. I was proud to tell them how well the TBM had served me on the journey, and that I had landed the airplane at Beijing Capital International Airport.

Everyone was curious to know whether China would open its airspace and what the future holds for general aviation in the country. It is probably the largest potential aviation market in the world. People knew there were a lot of challenges ahead but remained optimistic, especially when they learned that the government had let a small single-engine airplane land at Beijing Capital International Airport.

Numerous air shows were performed daily by the world's best aerobatic pilots. Aircraft manufacturers bring their best airplanes to the show and display their newest innovations. Equipment suppliers make their best offers to attendees. Best of all, we could see all kinds of airplanes, some just normal ones like ours, others were one of a kind. Rob, Shawn, and I spent every day going through the different camps: Warbirds, Vintage Airplanes, Ultra-light airplanes, Homebuilt airplanes, Light Sports Airplanes (LSA), and Seaplanes. At night, we stayed at the campground, where celebrations were hosted by various organizations and lasted until midnight. That was the most enjoyable week of the whole trip.

After five days of pure aviation fun around in Oshkosh, I was ready to finish my mission. I was ready to go home.

On July 29, 2011, Rob and I took off at 10 a.m., on a direct route to Memphis.

I love Memphis. When I was opening branches for my business, I had opportunities to live in other cities, including New York, Los

Angeles, and Houston, but they didn't feel quite like Memphis. Even when I lived in Flushing, New York, where I was surrounded by 60,000 Chinese and speaking English was optional, I never felt at home. What made Memphis home for me was the culture of southern hospitality.

In early 1996, I was searching for graduate schools in the U.S. for MBA study. My focus had always been international business. I applied to many schools and was accepted at a few notable ones, but none of them offered me the scholarship that I needed. Without an adequate scholarship, I would not have been able to afford the $20,000 to $30,000 per year tuition, not to mention living expenses.

In May 1996, while I was desperately hoping for a scholarship, I was accepted into the International MBA program at the University of Memphis and offered a full scholarship. The school not only waived my tuition, it also gave me a monthly stipend of $250, not a huge amount but enough to pay my rent. Coming to Memphis was the only financially viable choice I had.

When I decided to go to Memphis in 1996, my friends asked if I knew anyone there. All I knew about Memphis was Elvis and FedEx – that was about it. I arrived in August and in the first week I met two people who would become the most important individuals in my life, John and Isabel.

Because I didn't know anyone in the city, I called the University of Memphis Student Center to ask for help. The center gave me contact information for the President of the Chinese Student Association, who at the time was John Chen. So I called John, who had the same last name as me, just hoping that he might agree to pick me up and help me find a place to stay until I could get an apartment. I didn't realize that this phone call would lead to the best friend I've ever had.

John not only helped me find a place to stay for free, but he also spent days helping me find an apartment. He showed me around campus and all the "tricks" for how to get a free lunch and T-shirts while the school was welcoming new students.

We stayed close during my two years at the school. My apartment was his usual hang-out as it was close to campus. His home was my favorite place to enjoy authentic Chinese food cooked by his mom. John was hardworking and industrious. He got a job at a restaurant while he was in high school and paid his own way through college. When he was old enough, he worked as a bartender at a Japanese restaurant, Benihana, where he made great tips with his smile and friendly attitude. I would sometimes visit him to enjoy "free" cocktails when he was not so busy. We even backpacked through Europe together. When Isabel and I married, he was the best man and his fiancée was the maid of honor. Because we share the same last name, we often refer to each other as the "brother from another mother."

In the first week of school, there were many parties welcoming new students, many of whom left family behind and didn't have many friends in the new city. At one party organized just for new Chinese students, I noticed a tall and thin, shy girl. I walked over to her and introduced myself. We started chatting in Chinese. She told me her name was Zhaohui Xu, but she went by Isabel, because most Americans didn't know how to pronounce her given name. She was from Harbin, China, 2,000 miles away from my hometown in

Changsha, and had a full scholarship at the University of Memphis pursuing a PhD in Biomedical Engineering.

It was fate that brought us to the same city in the same week when our birth places were 2,000 miles apart. We started dating and fell in love not long after we met. Neither of us had relatives in Memphis. We helped and supported each other while pursuing our degrees. After dating for two years, we got married right before I graduated.

From the day I arrived in Memphis, I was embraced by my adopted hometown. The city has given me so much: my wonderful wife, my business partner, my education at the University of Memphis, and the opportunity to start and succeed at my own business. My heart was full of a great sense of appreciation and deep gratitude. Despite coming from such a faraway place, not speaking English well, and having such a different culture, Memphis welcomed and embraced me. I had come with nothing, and now I am so much richer than I'd ever imagined in all ways – in friendship, in family, in business.

The flight from Oshkosh to Memphis was short, about an hour and a half, and I had to go around a few summer thunderstorms. I knew people were waiting for us at the airport, but I was stunned by the high-level reception organized by Jon Thompson of the Memphis Airport Authority. Two fire trucks made a water bridge for my airplane to taxi under. Not only was my whole family there, 300 to 400 people were waiting at the hangar of Wilson Air Center, where the send-off benefit for St. Jude Children's Research Hospital was held.

After I shut down the engine, I took a deep breath and opened the door. There was a roar of cheers from the crowd and shouts of "Congratulations!" As Rob and I stepped out of the airplane, Isabel brought our three beautiful daughters to the plane with flowers in their hands. I hugged each one happily. My mom and dad had come back to the U.S. and gave me hugs as well. I knew that my mom was finally relieved from her worries over the past 70 days and that she had prayed every day to send blessings.

It was hot and humid in Memphis in late July after the rain. I was perspiring heavily, not just because of the weather, but also because of my excitement at the unexpected reception.

Memphis City Mayor A. C. Wharton Jr. and Shelby County Mayor Mark Luttrell are good friends of mine. They gave wonderful speeches about the trip on behalf of the city of Memphis and Shelby County. Greater Memphis Chamber President John Moore, who is also a great friend, delivered a speech on behalf of the Memphis business community. Richard Shadyac, Jr., CEO at ALSAC/St. Jude Children's Research Hospital, thanked me for my endeavor to raise awareness and money for St. Jude. Robert Wang, a self-made Chinese entrepreneur and big supporter of the journey, described how proud he felt about the trip. John Chen, who is also Chairman of Greater Memphis United Chinese Association, spoke on behalf of all Chinese in the greater Memphis area. Earl Blankenship shared his experience of flying with me in China and witnessing the historic part of the flight.

Also at the reception was world-renowned aviator, Elgen Long. Mr. Long set 15 aviation records. The first was his 1971 flight around the world over both poles. Special for me, it was the year

I was born. At age 84, he flew from Reno, Nevada, to give me an award: my official membership in the "Earthrounders" club.

At the end of the reception, I was asked to give a speech. I recalled how just before I flew back to Memphis, *The Commercial Appeal* carried an article about the trip, calling me a "hero." All I could say was, "I'm not a hero. I'm just a regular Memphis citizen who's been blessed by the community's support to be able to accomplish my dream."

I will never forget that moment of my life. I knew how very blessed and lucky I was. As the realization ran through me, I cried.

BEIJING TO MEMPHIS

From top to bottom: checking fuel quality in Russia;
aviation event in Oshkosh, WI; last stop in Oshkosh

Greeted by Memphis police officers at the end of the trip

Reception in Memphis

CHAPTER NINE

WHAT'S NEXT?

Whether you think you can, or you think you can't — you're right.

- Henry Ford

efore I came to Memphis, I'd been aware of two things the city was famous for: Elvis Presley, the King, was one. FedEx, founded by Frederick Smith, was the other. On August 4, 2011, six days after I finished my trip, I got an email from Mr. Smith.

He congratulated me on accomplishing this mission and asked if it would be possible to speak to me by phone. Of course it was possible – it was more than possible – it would be my great honor and privilege to speak with Mr. Smith, the brilliant entrepreneur I most admired.

We made an appointment for 2 p.m. the next day. On the dot on Friday, August 5, 2011, my phone rang. I nervously picked it up: "Is this Mr. Smith?" He answered, "Yes. Don't call me Mr.

Smith, call me Fred." I said, "Okay, Mr. Smith." I just couldn't call him "Fred." In Chinese culture, we always call the most respected people by their last name. Even though I have lived in the U.S. for 16 years, I still couldn't use his first name, at least not when speaking with him directly.

We went on to have a great conversation. He put me at ease when he talked about my airplane. His knowledge of aviation and airplanes amazed me. He even pointed out how reliable the PT6 engine on my airplane was. He asked me whether I had been in a big airplane, and I told him only as a passenger. He arranged a Boeing 777 Simulator flight for me. Being at the controls of a 766,000-pound flying machine was an awesome experience for a pilot with only 600 hours of flight time.

Frederick Smith has long been a legend to me as an entrepreneur. His success inspired a lot of people to start their own businesses, including myself.

Smith was born in Marks, Mississippi on August 11, 1944 and named after his father: James Frederick Smith. His father passed away when he was 4 year old, and he was raised by his mom and uncle. During his teenage years, he developed a love of airplanes, receiving his pilot's license at the age of 15 and flew crop dusters part time. In 1962, Smith entered Yale University and joined the Aviation Society of Yale. After graduation, he joined the U.S. Marine Corps, serving three years, from 1966 to 1969, as a platoon leader and a forward air controller (FAC), flying in the back seat of an OV-10. He served two tours of duty in Vietnam, flying on more than 200 combat missions. He was honorably discharged in 1969 with the rank of Captain, having received the Silver Star, the Bronze Star, and two Purple Hearts.

While attending Yale, he wrote a paper for an economic class, outlining overnight delivery service in a computer information age. It was modeled on bank clearing houses, but instead of settling financial transactions of satellite banks at a central location, physical goods would be sent for delivery to designated addresses. His professor gave him a "C" on his paper due to the infeasibility of this idea.

The story of how Smith started FedEx resonated with the central question: "What would you attempt to do if you knew you couldn't fail?"

He started a business despite the fact that his professor didn't consider the idea behind FedEx feasible and gave him a C on the paper. If someone like a Yale professor told you, at the age of 20, that your idea was crazy and unfeasible, probably 99.9 percent of us would drop the idea and move on. What did we, as freshman students, know about the real world?

Nevertheless, Smith started Federal Express on June 18, 1971 at the age of 27, with $4 million inheritance and an additional $91 million in venture capital. In 1973, the company began service in 25 cities. It started with small packages and documents and a fleet of 14 Falcon 20 (DA-20) jets. The company went public in 1978. Now FedEx employs more than 300,000 people worldwide, owns and operates more than 600 airplanes, and generates about $40 billion in annual revenue.

It takes absolute courage to stand up and believe in yourself and your dream. It takes even more courage to gamble your life savings on making it come true. Mr. Smith not only "gambled" everything on his idea, he also revolutionized industry and changed the world with a tool that today many of us can't function without. Can you imagine a world without FedEx? I cannot.

I have been using Verne Harnish's book *Mastering the Rockefeller Habits* to manage my company for more than six years. This allowed me to call the office only once during my 69-day trip, and the company's management grew the business more than 30 percent that year. Once a year in the U.S., Verne hosts a Fortune Leadership Summit. I was invited by my business partner, Steve Sansom, to join one being held in Atlanta, Georgia, May 15 to 16, 2012. Jim Collins was the keynote speaker, and I was excited at the prospect of seeing him for the first time. As you know by now, his theories have influenced me greatly not just in business but in every area of my life. So I was eager to see this man who was considered "the greatest business thinker of all time."

During the break after his marvelous speech on his and Morten T. Hansen's book, *Great by Choice*, I walked over to him, shook his hand and told him he had saved my life. His eyebrow raised a little, and he said in his characteristically calm way, "How?"

I told him how his theories of the 20 Mile March and a Culture of Discipline helped me accomplish my trip. I knew that I couldn't have finished it if I didn't stick with the 20 Mile March theory, and that I might not have started at all, if I had been cowed by the volcanic eruption in Iceland. I knew that I could not have completed the journey without a Culture of Discipline and an unrelenting inner determination.

I went to bed before 9 p.m. every night no matter how much distraction came from the media or friends' hospitality. I fueled the airplane myself as soon as we landed at every stop to make sure the fuel was good and we were ready to go the next day. I made a pre-flight check with strict discipline before each takeoff. I landed at every small airport with a disciplined approach, and applied the same principle to every careful step I took to ensure success.

He appeared pleased to hear this story and congratulated me on my accomplishment. He was named after his grandfather, Jimmy Collins, who was the chief test pilot for the Grumman military aircraft company during the 1930s. His grandfather, who died in a crash while testing the F3 Biplane, had actually predicted and described his death before it occurred. On December 8, 2010, Jim Collins republished an autobiography entitled *Test Pilot*, written by his grandfather in 1935.

One of Jim Collins's most important business concepts is Return on Luck. I consider myself to be an extremely lucky individual. I have been fortunate to fulfill three dreams in my 40 years. I was lucky to stay healthy in childhood, lucky to get a U.S. visa, lucky to get a scholarship at the University of Memphis, lucky to meet Isabel and John, lucky to start my business and find a niche in scaffold products, and lucky to fly around the world. I could name many, many more instances. However, the real question is, am I luckier than others? Or did I just get a high return on these lucky events?

I also had a lot of bad luck in my life. I was born during China's Cultural Revolution when food was scarce and schools were being closed. I fought in the streets at a young age. I had bad luck in my first visa application. I had catastrophic quality problems in the early stage of my business, and I encountered one of the worst financial crises in history in 2008 when the real estate bubble burst. My business was heavily exposed to the construction market. In my flight around the world, I was faced with a volcanic eruption, airplane problems, the most frightening flight of my life in an Indian monsoon, violent turbulence in Vietnam, and many other difficulties.

Luck, good and bad, happens to everyone. High achievers recognize good luck, seize it, and are able to get greater returns from it. I was not the only one who got a U.S. visa. I was not the only Chinese student to receive a scholarship to a university. I was not the only one who tried to import scaffolds to the U.S. Certainly, I was not the only Chinese pilot to attempt a historic flight.

When these lucky events happened, I recognized them, seized the opportunity, and got the best return on my luck.

I'm often asked, "What's next?" My answer is that I am passionate about two things: children's charities and China's general aviation.

I know how blessed I was as a kid to have enough food in the midst of China's Cultural Revolution, to have stayed relatively healthy, and to have had the opportunity to get an education. There are still millions of children born today into similarly challenging conditions. They need help with basic needs, including food, medicine, and education.

If you care enough to look, you'll see unfortunate children are not just in rural areas of developing countries, such as India,

China, and Africa, many live just around the corner from well-to-do families in communities worldwide. They may have food, but their lives will not change without adequate education.

As adults, we make choices in our lives and bear the consequence, good or bad. However, children don't have the same options. They are born into situations not of their choosing. They are not old enough to decide what to eat, what hospital they go to when they get sick, or what school they should attend.

As parents and caring adults, our obligation starts with the birth of a child, to make sure that child is well cared for until he or she is old enough to make good choices. If parents cannot afford this, our society and community ought to do whatever possible to help. Government is limited as to what it can do. As citizens, you and I can give whatever we can afford, even if it's just helping one child at a time in our own communities. One mission of my flight, to raise money for St. Jude Children's Research Hospital, didn't end when my trip ended. It remains a lifelong goal to help more children around the world, such as the elementary students in Laos and the orphans in Vietnam.

I enjoy the freedom of flying in the U.S. regularly. It has become part of my life. Chinese people don't lack a passion for flying. After all, the kite was invented in China 2,800 years ago. With 1.3 billion people and growing wealth, dreams of the freedom to fly live in the hearts of many Chinese. I have heard stories that some farmers have built their own flying machines using a basic steel structure, motor, and propeller. They want to fly! However, airspace remains restricted by military.

I remain highly optimistic about the future of China's general aviation. On August 23, 2012, after approval from China's Central Military Commission and the State Council, China opened the country's airspace to altitudes lower than 1,000 meters. That decision is a beginning, but there are still many things to do to build a market-oriented infrastructure for private pilots in China. Airports will need to establish fixed base operators, fuel supplies, maintenance facilities, radar service, flight training, and many other services and facilities.

Airplanes are easy to buy. With the slowing aviation industry in the U.S. and other developed countries, airplane manufacturers struggle to sell new planes. China will be the largest potential market in the world. The U.S. has more than 600,000 pilots but China has only about 30,000 of which a mere 1,000 are private pilots. To build a general aviation market, the top priority is to foster more pilots not just commercial airline pilots, but private aviators.

The best way to get people interested in flying is to take them up and show them what an airplane can do. My passion for aviation goes beyond its use as a transportation tool. I enjoy aerobatic flying, pushing an airplane's capability to fly like a bird at different angles, speeds, and positions. Aerobatic flying not only makes me a better and safer pilot, it also lets me experience the real joy of flight.

At this infant stage of private flying in China, aerobatic flying is almost nonexistent. I've found a new passion in my desire to bring this experience to China and to provide the opportunity for private pilots to experience the pure joy of flight. Since I finished my trip around the world in 2011, I have been working on the "Flying Dragons Aerobatic Team" and hope to debut with it in China's largest general aviation show in Xi'an.

My journey taught me many things, but foremost is to dream big and to pursue that Big Hairy Audacious Goal. Big or small, we need dreams. They're essential to a great life. Many of us give up our dreams because we are afraid of failure.

We all tend to stay in our comfort zone. Starting as kids, our loving parents want us to follow the rules and make sure we don't get hurt. When we try something new, we automatically evaluate the chance for success. If we don't feel comfortable, then we consider it a bad or stupid idea. We fear failure and the prospect of looking foolish. However, if we stay in our comfort zones, there is no room for adventure and excitement.

Those willing to take risks will be those who will reap the biggest rewards. When I started the company on credit card debt, I was scared and uncertain, but also alert, focused, and disciplined. That endeavor lay far outside of my comfort zone. It was almost unnerving, but at the same time exhilarating and invigorating. It was one of the most exciting times of my life.

When I started planning my RTW trip I had only 500 flying hours, and I had the same unease as when I started my business.

Looking back, every time I have stepped out of my comfort zone and tried something "crazy," I have been rewarded beyond my imagination. Those times have made my life more meaningful.

My children were too young when I took my trip to understand much about it. When they grow old enough to ask intelligent questions, I will answer and then return a question:

"What would you attempt to do if you knew you could not fail?"

Meeting Jim Collins

Meeting Fred Smith

Collage of photos from the trip

APPENDIX I

THE ROUTE

May, 22nd, 2011	Memphis to Washington, D.C.
May 23rd, 2011	Washington, D.C. to Toronto, Canada
May 25th, 2011	Toronto, Canada to Quebec City, Canada
May 27th, 2011	Quebec City, Canada to Schefferville, Canada
May 27th, 2011	Schefferville, Canada to Nuuk, Greenland
May 28th, 2011	Nuuk, Greenland to Reykjavik, Iceland
May 29th, 2011	Reykjavik, Iceland to Edinburgh, Scotland
May 30th, 2011	Edinburgh, Scotland to Stonehenge, England
May 31st, 2011	Stonehenge, England to Paris, France
June 3rd, 2011	Paris, France to Madrid, Spain
June 6th, 2011	Madrid, Spain to Barcelona, Spain
June 8th, 2011	Barcelona, Spain to Tarbes, France
June 8th, 2011	Tarbes, France to Milan, Italy
June 10th, 2011	Milan, Italy to Rome, Italy
June 12th, 2011	Rome, Italy to Athens, Greece
June 14th, 2011	Athens, Greece to Limassol, Cyprus
June 16th, 2011	Limassol, Cyprus to Hail, Saudi Arabia

June 16th, 2011	Hail, Saudi Arabia to Dubai, UAE
June 23rd, 2011	Dubai, UAE to Muscat, Oman
June 24th, 2011	Muscat, Oman to Ahmedabad, India
June 24th, 2011	Ahmedabad, India to Agra, India
June 27th, 2011	Agra, India to Kolkata, India
June 28th, 2011	Kolkata, India to Bangkok, Thailand
June 30th, 2011	Bangkok, Thailand to Vientiane, Laos
July 2nd, 2011	Vientiane, Laos to Ho Chi Minh City, Vietnam
July 4th, 2011	Ho Chi Minh City, Vietnam to Hong Kong
July 7th, 2011	Hong Kong to Changsha
July 10th, 2011	Changsha, China to Xi'an China
July 12th, 2011	Xi'an, China to Beijing, China
July 15th, 2011	Beijing, China to Harbin, China
July 17th, 2011	Harbin, China to Khabarovsk, Russia
July 18th, 2011	Khabarovsk, Russia to Magadan, Russia
July 18th, 2011	Magadan, Russia to Anadyr, Russia
July 19th/18th, 2011	Anadyr, Russia to Anchorage, AK (Gained one day)
July 20th, 2011	Anchorage, AK to Juneau, AK
July 20th, 2011	Juneau, AK to Seattle, WA
July 22nd, 2011	Seattle, WA to Los Angeles, CA
July 24th, 2011	Los Angeles, CA to Oshkosh, WI
July 29th, 2011	Oshkosh, WI to Memphis, TN

TOP TEN THINGS EVERY ROUND-THE-WORLD PILOT SHOULD KNOW

1. Check the fuel quality and fuel the airplane by yourself as soon as you land.

2. Always fly in the daytime and check airport operational schedules.

3. Eat carefully and sleep soundly.

4. Hire local handlers in the Middle East and Asian countries.

5. Carry at least $20,000 U.S. dollars in cash and hide it in the airplane.

6. Obtain adequate insurance required for landing permits.

7. Learn the local flight rules and adopt them quickly.

8. Talk to the local pilots whenever possible. They have the most knowledge about the local flying conditions.

9. Speak slowly and clearly when talking to ATC in non-English speaking countries.

10. Do not assume you'll always get the tailwind by flying eastward.

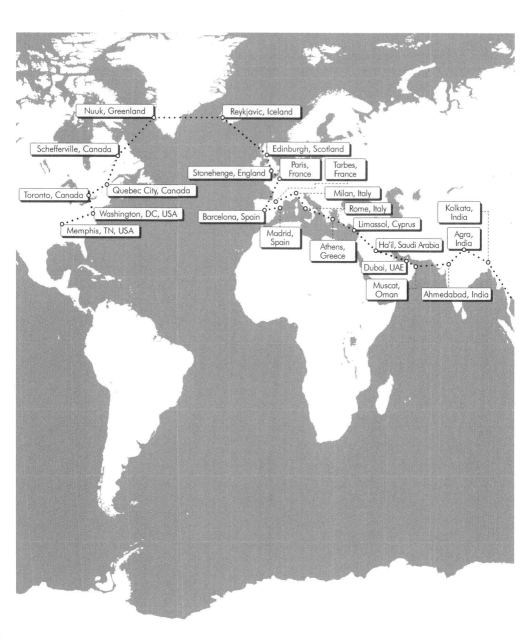

Nuuk, Greenland

Reykjavic, Iceland

Schefferville, Canada

Edinburgh, Scotland

Stonehenge, England

Paris, France

Tarbes, France

Toronto, Canada

Quebec City, Canada

Milan, Italy

Kolkata, India

Washington, DC, USA

Barcelona, Spain

Rome, Italy

Memphis, TN, USA

Limassol, Cyprus

Agra, India

Madrid, Spain

Ha'il, Saudi Arabia

Athens, Greece

Dubai, UAE

Muscat, Oman

Ahmedabad, India

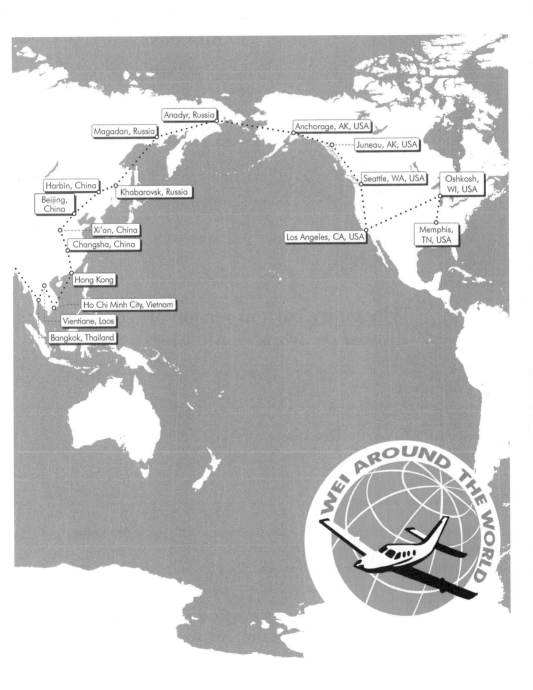

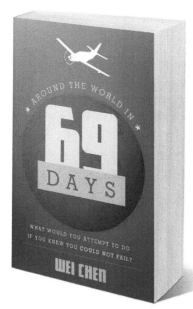

How can you use this book?

MOTIVATE

EDUCATE

THANK

INSPIRE

PROMOTE

CONNECT

Why have a custom version of *Around the World in 69 Days?*

- Build personal bonds with customers, prospects, employees, donors, and key constituencies
- Develop a long-lasting reminder of your event, milestone, or celebration
- Provide a keepsake that inspires change in behavior and change in lives
- Deliver the ultimate "thank you" gift that remains on coffee tables and bookshelves
- Generate the "wow" factor

Books are thoughtful gifts that provide a genuine sentiment that other promotional items cannot express. They promote employee discussions and interaction, reinforce an event's meaning or location, and they make a lasting impression. Use your book to say "Thank You" and show people that you care.

Around the World in 69 Days is available in bulk quantities and in customized versions at special discounts for corporate, institutional, and educational purposes. To learn more please contact our Special Sales team at:

1.866.775.1696 • sales@advantageww.com • www.AdvantageSpecialSales.com

CPSIA information can be obtained at www.ICGtesting.com
Printed in the USA
LVOW01s0707031113

359740LV00004B/5/P